IN
KENT

Janet Cameron

COUNTRYSIDE BOOKS
NEWBURY BERKSHIRE

First published 2007
© Janet Cameron, 2007

COUNTRYSIDE BOOKS
3 Catherine Road
Newbury, Berkshire

To view our complete range of books,
please visit us at
www.countrysidebooks.co.uk

ISBN 978 1 84674 027 5

*With thanks to my sister, Lin Campbell
and my friends, Sylvia Kent and Caroline Cash
for all their support*

Photographs by the author unless stated otherwise
Maps by Gelder Design & Mapping

Cover picture supplied by Faith Tillotson

Designed by Peter Davies, Nautilus Design
Produced through MRM Associates Ltd., Reading
Typeset by Jean Cussons Typesetting, Diss, Norfolk
Printed by Cambridge University Press

Contents

PUBLISHER'S NOTE

We hope that you obtain considerable enjoyment from this book; great care has been taken in its preparation. Although at the time of publication all routes followed public rights of way or permitted paths, diversion orders can be made and permissions withdrawn.

We cannot, of course, be held responsible for such diversion orders and any inaccuracies in the text which result from these or any other changes to the routes nor any damage which might result from walkers trespassing on private property. We are anxious, though, that all details covering the walks are kept up to date and would therefore welcome information from readers which would be relevant to future editions.

The simple sketch maps that accompany the walks in this book are based on notes made by the author whilst checking out the routes on the ground. However, for the benefit of a proper map, we do recommend that you purchase the relevant Ordnance Survey sheet covering your walk. The Ordnance Survey maps are widely available, especially through booksellers and local newsagents.

Introduction

Here are twenty enjoyable walks with lots to see and do with your children. They range from short, easy circuits of a mile or less, taking in country parks with child-friendly attractions, and longer, more challenging walks of two or three miles for adventurous, older children. Walk near the seaside, along lovely waterways, through woodlands and across wide-open spaces with stunning views. The book contains suggestions of what the children might look out for so they can improve their knowledge of natural history while they flex their walking muscles.

There is a section on refreshments to help you decide whether to take a picnic or eat out and an indication as to whether the walk is suitable for buggies. Telephone numbers are listed for you to check the latest information about opening times of attractions and refreshment stops. Short stretches of lane-walking are sometimes necessary to connect one part of a walk to another. Although these lanes are generally quiet, take care to watch out for passing traffic. Comfortable footwear is also a must, as well as long trousers to protect legs from possible nettle and insect stings.

Two of the walks, Great Chart and Upstreet (Stodmarsh), are half-linear, half-circular – this is due to the network of unbridged waterways or poorly-maintained bridges which preclude a safe, full circuit. These are particularly stunning walks and it would have been a pity not to include them.

All the routes have been carefully plotted and checked and a sketch map accompanies each one but please remember that the landscape can change – paths become overgrown, new fences may appear and footpaths may be diverted. It's a good idea, therefore, to carry the relevant OS map, details of which are also given.

So go well prepared and enjoy these walks through some of the most beautiful countryside Kent has to offer. I wish you and your children happy, healthy walking.

Janet Cameron

AREA MAP SHOWING THE LOCATIONS OF THE WALKS

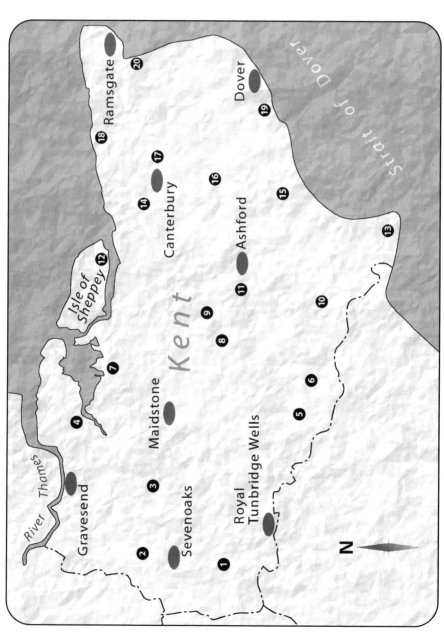

1

Bough Beech, near Sevenoaks

Mind the mice don't nick your nibbles

The reservoir at Bough Beech.

Near the old oast house, converted into a visitor centre, at Bough Beech, live lots of hungry field mice and Kent Wildlife Trust's leaflet carries a caution – to watch out for your food! This delightful walk takes you along the causeway, with views over the sparkling reservoir. Later, you will walk through woodlands and lovely meadows, and along grassy footpaths, with fine views across the countryside.

Kiddiwalks in Kent

1

Getting there *At Junction 5 of the M25, take the A21 south, turning right along the B2027. Bough Beech Visitor Centre is signposted off the B2027 east of Bough Beech village or off the B2042 south of Ide Hill, near Sevenoaks. Follow the 'brown duck' signs. The visitor centre is open from April to the end of October (Wednesday, Saturday, Sunday and bank holidays). When its car park is closed, you can park on the causeway and go to the centre on foot. Telephone: Kent Wildlife Trust on 01622 662012 for further details.*

Length of walk 2 miles.
Time 1½ to 2½ hours.
Terrain Comfortable walking. Moderately hilly in places, with a few stiles. Unsuitable for buggies except along the causeway.
Start/parking Bough Beech Visitor Centre situated off the causeway (GR 496494).
Map OS Explorer 147.
Refreshments Take your own picnic to eat in the open-sided barn at the visitor centre, where there are picnic benches.

◆ Fun Things to See and Do ◆

The causeway is a favourite haunt for birdwatchers interested in herons, cormorants, waders, terns, sparrowhawks and kestrels. Why not join them with your binoculars and see how many varieties of birds you can spot? You could take a field guide to help you identify them.

Kent Wildlife Trust, which operates the visitor centre, runs exciting events especially for children. Many events are at weekends, including pond dipping, studying rocks and fossils, woodcraft, bat-walking with a bat detector – and that's just a few. For further details, log onto www.kentwildlifetrust.org.uk

1 From the visitor centre car park return to the road (the causeway) and turn right. Enjoy views over the reservoir spread out on either side. You may see cormorants and herons on the shore and small islands. As you leave the reservoir behind you, find the public footpath signpost, beside a wooden noticeboard that says 'Commonwork Field Trail'.

Turning left, climb the stile in the hedgerow onto the footpath.

2 Start ascending through woods. Shortly, climb another stile and continue ahead, still gently ascending and passing a red and yellow banded post on your left. Go ahead through an intersection of widely-spaced trees, passing another red and

The Walk

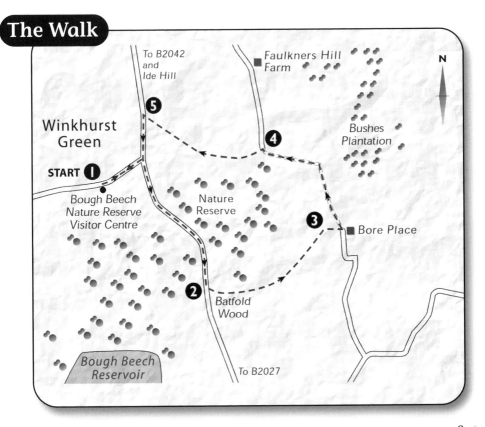

◆◆◆***1***◆◆◆◆◆◆◆◆◆◆◆◆◆◆◆◆◆◆◆◆◆◆◆◆◆◆◆◆◆◆◆◆

Enjoying the view over the reservoir.

yellow banded post on your left. Continue with woods to your left and a meadow on your right. At a facing hedgerow, bear left along a track, and climb the stile beside a metal gate. Aim for three large trees in a hedgerow on the other side of the field.

❸ On reaching the three large trees, bear right, so the hedgerow runs to your left. Continue for a short way to a stile with a red and yellow banded post beside a gate ahead. Climb the stile and go

along a short track, past the farm buildings, immediately turning left onto a farm track. Follow the track, curving around a left bend. The track continues to curve, but keep to it, ignoring yellow arrow markers on the way.

❹ Just before the track turns right, you'll see a waymarker pointing diagonally left on a large tree trunk beside a stile and gate. Climb the stile and follow the direction of the waymarker through the field. At a facing tree line, bear right. Soon you'll spot the reservoir on your left. Follow this curving footpath. Turn left at an opening between hedges (ignoring a metal gate immediately on your left) and cross a plank bridge. Continue ahead with a fence on your left, gently ascending.

5 At the end of the footpath, go through a gap beside a metal gate, and turn left into a lane, watching for traffic. There's a narrow grass verge on the left which you can use for most of the way. When it runs out, it might be safer to cross the road for the last few yards, facing possible oncoming traffic. Turn right at the Bough Beech Visitor Centre signpost, retracing your steps back to the start.

◆ Background Notes ◆

The oast house at Bough Beech Visitor Centre is all that remains of old Winkhurst Farm. The farmhouse itself was dismantled and relocated near Chichester, at the Weald and Downland Museum, which is an open-air site for about 50 historic buildings. Winkhurst farmhouse was moved in 1968 to avoid contamination of the reservoir and it was re-erected at its new site the following year. Historians dated it at around 1492–1537, and now believe it might have been a kitchen area, attached to a larger house.

Bough Beech Reservoir draws its supplies from the River Eden. About 150 species of birds have been recorded regularly, including ospreys and waders, and recently, the little crake made an appearance. A floating island helps sustain the terns, while sheep graze the banks to maintain the grass.

Bore Place, near Bough Beech, is a dairy farm, covering 500 acres. In 1977, a group of rural enterprise and educational charitable trusts set up the Commonwork project, to improve the land for wildlife and people (see Commonwork Field Trail at the end of point 1 of the walk).

2

Lullingstone Country Park

Where knights enjoyed a joust

Paddling in the stream at the start of the walk.

This is a lovely, riverside stroll, where you can enjoy the dappled beauty of the sun filtering through the greenery in summer and, over the water, the dragonflies buzzing about their business. A gentle climb to the brow of a ridge follows, where there are magnificent views over the surrounding countryside. Nearby Eynsford is a popular, quaint village with plenty to see. Look out for the tilt yard at Lullingstone Castle, where in days gone by jousting took place and, if you want to, you can wade through the ford across the stream but make sure you're wearing your wellies!

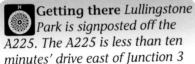

Getting there *Lullingstone Park is signposted off the A225. The A225 is less than ten minutes' drive east of Junction 3 of the M25. The park is also less than half a mile south of Eynsford railway station.*

Length of walk 1¼ miles.
Time 1 hour.
Terrain Gentle uphill climbing halfway round the walk. The riverside section is fine for buggies. The walk is a little bumpy on the short uphill stretch.
Start/parking Lullingstone Visitor Centre where there is an honesty box (GR 526638).
Map OS Explorer 147.
Refreshments Picnic area available. Lullingstone Country Park Visitor Centre serves a variety of hot and cold drinks and snacks. Telephone: 01322 865995.

The Walk

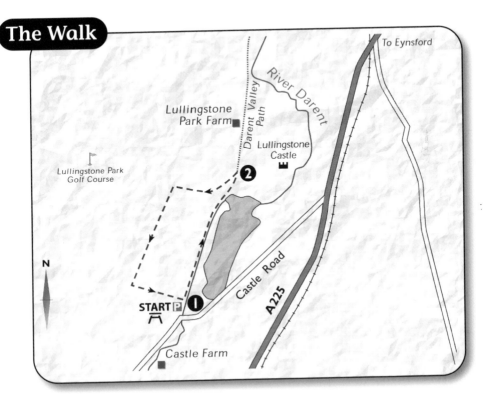

Kiddiwalks in Kent

1 Turn right out of the visitor centre, go through a gap in a hedge and turn right towards the River Darent, passing through the picnic area. Go through a kissing gate, turn left and follow the lovely riverside path to the end. Pass through another kissing

On the riverside path.

◆ Fun Things to See and Do ◆

If you take wellies, it is shallow enough, with adult supervision, for the children to paddle across the stream close to the little bridge at the start of the walk. They may want to take their fishing nets along too.

A visit to nearby Lullingstone Castle is also an option, with its unique and wonderful plant garden.

gate. You will see Lullingstone Castle ahead on your right. Just before reaching the castle, turn left along a tarmac track opposite the weir and begin gently ascending.

2 The field on your right is the tilt yard (see *Background Notes*). Continue towards a row of trees facing you across the brow of the hill. Turn left in front of this tree line and continue, following the grassy footpath, with glorious views to your left, and later also opening up to your right. Go slightly uphill, then begin descending. At the end of the path, bear left, back to the visitor centre.

◆ Background Notes ◆

Lullingstone Castle, which you will glimpse at point 2 of the walk, is a medieval family mansion where Henry VIII and Queen Anne have both stayed. It features a World Garden of Plants that has been created by the plant-hunter Tom Hart Dyke. In 2002 Tom Hart Dyke was kidnapped while on a plant-hunt and held hostage by guerrillas for nine months in the Colombian jungle and that is where he first had his vision for a World Garden of Plants. Every year new and rare plants are added to its collection and it includes a Wollemi Pine, popularly known as the dinosaur tree. The dinosaur tree near Ayers Rock in Australia is thought to be the oldest tree in the world. In 2006, a beautiful eucalyptus Silver Princess actually flowered for the first time in the United Kingdom in Lullingstone Castle's garden.

When you reach point 2 of the walk and begin to climb the small hill, look to your right. In this meadow there was once a **'tilt yard'** – meaning a place where knights practised jousting. Even further back in history, these lower parts were a huge swamp and early Britons lived on the higher ground you see ahead as you climb. People using metal detectors have found interesting artefacts in the area and some are on show in Lullingstone Castle, including a jousting helmet. Telephone for further details: 01322 862114 or visit the website: www.lullingstonecastle.co.uk

3

Trosley Country Park

Tone-up on the trim trail

The visitor centre at Trosley.

his is a terrific walk through part of a superb country park, with the added attraction of a chance to tone up your muscles! Trosley Country Park is very user-friendly, with lovely picnic areas dotted around and a 'trim trail' offering exciting pieces of equipment, probably best suited to slightly older children – also ideal for adults. So, if you'd like to lose a few pounds (and who wouldn't!) while enjoying a woodland walk, with some great views on the return section, you can't do better than Trosley. The return journey is famous for its swathes of bluebells – but even if it's not bluebell time, there's plenty for everyone to enjoy.

Getting there *Trosley Country Park, Waterlow Road, Meopham, is clearly signposted off the A227 (Gravesend Road) near Meopham. The nearest motorway access is Junction 2 of the M20 or Junction 2A of the M26.*

Length of walk 1½ miles.
Time 1 to 1½ hours.
Terrain Comfortable, mostly level, footpath walking. Buggies at your discretion; there are some bumpy patches along pebbled tracks.
Start/parking Trosley Country Park Visitor Centre (GR 632611).
Map OS Explorer 148.
Refreshments Trosley Country Park Visitor Centre offers a variety of hot and cold snacks and drinks, with plenty of tables and chairs both outside and in. There are modern baby-changing and disabled facilities adjacent to the centre. Telephone: 01732 823570. Website: www.kentdowns.org.uk

The Walk

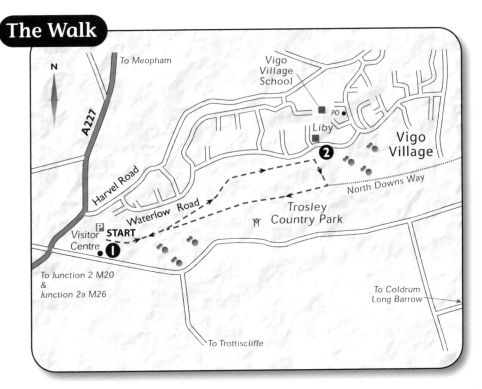

Kiddiwalks in Kent

1 After parking in one of the several parking bays, make your way to the visitor centre. Beside a large signboard adjacent to the centre, find the trim trail signpost and follow the arrow ahead. Go past Ladderwalk on your left, continuing ahead past Chin-Ups. Pass between posts beside a metal gate, perhaps stopping to try the Hurdles, also on the left. Now continue through woods, ignoring paths to the right, following the waymarked route through the gap by the metal gate. Leapfrog is your next challenge! Almost immediately after passing Step-Ups turn right.

2 Walk along this woodland path, stopping to flex your muscles on the Arm Stretch. When you reach a T-junction, turn right. This section is designated part of the trim trail and the Blue Walk, so named to show Trosley's pride in the magnificent bluebell display. On your left are the Parallel Bars and later the Balance Beam. Keep

◆ Fun Things to See and Do ◆

See how many different kinds of leaves you can collect. Trosley is famous for its beautiful trees, and especially for its oaks. If you don't have one already, borrow a tree identification book from the library and see if you can name all the leaves you have gathered. You could even make a sculpture of your leaves by putting some greaseproof paper onto a table, and then placing some modelling dough on top. You can make your dough whatever shape you wish, round, square, oblong or oval, then roll it out to about 5 mm thick. Carefully arrange your leaves on the dough in an attractive pattern, and use the roller to press them into the dough. When you lift them off, they will have left a lovely pattern behind.

On the way to the trim trail.

straight ahead, looking out for the Sit-Ups equipment, partially hidden behind bushes. Shortly, make the most of the last trim trail attraction, the Pole-Climb on your right. On your left, down some steps, is a wonderful picnic site, with picnic tables and benches. Continue in the same direction and at a Trosley information board, turn immediately right, slightly uphill a few yards, back to the visitor centre.

◆ Background Notes ◆

'Trosley' is a shortened version of Trottiscliffe, the name of a nearby village. The park covers 170 acres and lies on the North Downs Ridge. The Pilgrims' Way, which uses the same route as the North Downs Way, runs through Trosley Country Park. It is an ancient road used by pilgrims travelling between Winchester and Canterbury.

A Neolithic monument, the Coldrum Long Barrow, can be found nearby, just off the Pilgrims' Way. You can park off Pinesfield Lane to the east of Trottiscliffe village and take a footpath to view the remains of this ancient burial chamber, said to date from 4,000 BC.

4

Shorne Wood Country Park

A walk, a hop, a skip and a jump!

Shorne's famous Faerie Ring.

These two walks are a delight for all the family as there's lots to do in a stunning landscape of woodlands, winding footpaths and meadows and a super trim trail to try out – a real treat! Also, there's plenty of water around, everything from fishing lakes and lovely wildlife ponds to a dogs' dipping pond! Most people seem to like this pond best, as dogs always know exactly how to have fun and you can't help wanting to join in.

The shorter walk is suitable for buggies, but the longer one has a few hills to climb and steps to descend, although these are not too demanding for older children and adults. The reward for making the extra effort – some magnificent views along the way.

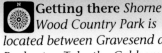 **Getting there** *Shorne Wood Country Park is located between Gravesend and Rochester. Take the Cobham/ Shorne/Higham junction off the A2 and follow the signs.*

Length of walk ¾ mile or 2½ miles.
Time Short walk: 45 mins to 1¼ hours; long walk: 2 to 3 hours.
Terrain Easy walking for the shorter, buggy walk. The longer walk has frequent, if short, uphill climbs and a number of descending steps.
Start/parking Shorne Wood Country Park (GR 683699).
Map OS Explorer 163.
Refreshments A variety of refreshments is available at the new visitor centre at the Country Park. Telephone: 01474 823800. Website: www.kent.gov.uk/ countrysideaccess

The Walk

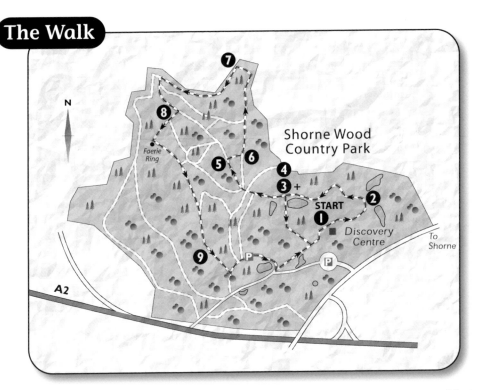

Kiddiwalks in Kent

Points (1) and (2) are for both the longer walk and the buggy walk. Thereafter, separate routes are clearly defined.

1 Leave the car park, passing the Discovery Centre and large information board on your left. Continue along a track between fences towards signboards and then turn right, towards Quarry Car Park and Furzy Leas Meadow. Follow the tree-lined footpath until you reach a wide path through open ground. The children might try the Leapfrog apparatus to the left, or maybe have some fun in the adventure playground on the right. Then continue as before, and just

◆ Fun Things to See and Do ◆

On the short walk, to increase your children's enjoyment and education, they might bring along a sketch pad and pencils so they can record the things they see. It could be fun watching and sketching the dogs in the dipping pool. An adventure playground, also accessible on the shorter route, is a bonus in this child-friendly area.

On the longer walk, children will enjoy using their binoculars especially at the Knoll, where there are fine views over the Thames estuary.

Close to the main car park area, children can see most of Kent's native trees, labelled for easy identification, and both walks end near the Sensory Garden, with its sculptures, scents and colour.

If you have an NRA rod licence, you may fish on the Furzy Leas Lakes from dawn to dusk. Day tickets can be purchased for a few pounds, half-price for children, telephone 01474 823800 for current prices.

before you reach the fishing lake signpost, turn left, waymarked on a wooden post.

2 After a few yards, turn left again at the Vault apparatus. Bear right past the Parallel Bar and almost immediately swing left past the Step-Ups. Continue through woodlands, mostly silver birch, and pass the Pole Climb on your left and then Chin-Ups. Older children can have some fun along this part of the walk, and even the little ones could join in on some of the apparatus, with adult assistance. Soon after passing Hurdles, you'll reach Shorne Dam Pond on your left, specially set aside for dogs to swim and fetch sticks from the water. Don't stand too close as I did, unless you want a cold, muddy shower as they shake themselves dry! Now decide which walk you want to take – (3) for the short walk, but if you want to take the longer route, omit (3) and go straight to (4).

3 *Buggy walk only* Turn left at the corner of the dogs' swimming pond. Soon, the pond gives way to a little stream running on your left. Pass Sit-Ups on your right and then go over a wooden bridge. Bear left and immediately cross another bridge. Follow the curving pathway over another wooden bridge. Pass the Ladderwalk on your left and the Balance Beam on your right. Soon, at a waymarked post, turn right into the Sensory Garden. After enjoying the garden, take an exit onto the main pathway running on the opposite side of the garden and turn left. Soon, look right and you will see the roof of the Discovery Centre through the trees. Follow the main signs back to the car park.

4 *For the longer walk* Ignore the footpath going sharply left around the pond. Bearing slightly left, you will see the red route waymarked ahead, passing over a wooden bridge. Cross the bridge and shortly bear right. Continue up a slight incline then begin to descend following the red arrows along the woodland footpath for a short distance. Ignore intersecting paths which are not waymarked. Soon, turn right at a wooden post, through mature woodland.

5 Shortly, at an intersection, turn right and descend, then begin to climb again, with a large hollow dropping down to your left. At the next T-junction of

There are plenty of wide open spaces at Shorne for the children to enjoy

paths, turn left. Soon, you will see delightful views of the valley to your left.

6 Shortly, bear left, descending down steps to the bottom. On reaching the bottom, turn left.

7 Continue, soon climbing uphill, eventually bearing left and still following the red arrows. Shortly, another waymarker will guide you to the right, with woodlands on your right and a large meadow to your left. Turn left at the top edge of the meadow. This is the Knoll, a famous place for the amazing views to your left, over the Thames estuary. At a wooden post by a silver birch tree, turn right.

8 Descend steps, waymarked with a red arrow. (This is Cardiac Hill, so take it easy!) At the bottom, you will find Shorne's famous Faerie Ring with its fascinating, sculptured seats. Younger children might enjoy sitting in the fairies' seats and holding council. Leaving the Faerie Ring, return to the main path, and turn right. (If you don't go into the Faerie Ring, turn left after descending Cardiac Hill, so the Faerie Ring is on your right.) Keep to this main path, bearing right through a number of tree stumps – or, if you still have enough energy, you can prove it by leaping from one to another! Then continue ahead along the undulating path. Almost immediately, bear right to Randal Bottom Pond, a peaceful, stretch of wildlife water, lying on your right.

9 Continue along this path, following the red arrows. Soon, cross a wooden bridge, then ascend a flight of about 20 steps. Aim for the Discovery Centre signpost ahead, and then turn left in front of it along a narrow footpath. Pass Wood Henge on your left, a resting place, and ponds on your right. Follow the curve to the right past the car park sign. After crossing a wooden bridge, you will see to your left the Sensory Gardens, with fine sculptures, including one of the Green Man.

After enjoying the garden, take an exit onto the main pathway running on the opposite side of the garden and turn left. Soon, look right and you will see the roof of the Discovery Centre through the trees. Follow the main signs back to the car park.

◆ Background Notes ◆

Shorne Wood Country Park is designated an Area of Outstanding Natural Beauty and, because of its abundant wildlife, a Site of Special Scientific Interest. The Cobham Hall Estate originally occupied the site and, between 1920 and 1970, clay was extracted from the area for making cement. In 1987, it was decided to open this landscaped haven to the public. Now it is owned by Kent County Council, assisted by Gravesham Borough Council. During the Great Storm of 1987, many trees were lost, but more have been planted, including rare and protected species.

The **Sensory Garden** has been specially created to affect all your senses, with colour, scent, texture, shape and sound. Its most important sculpture depicts the Green Man fighting off evil serpents and holding the world out of their reach to keep it safe. A worldwide symbol of fertility, the Green Man is also the spirit of the trees.

5

Goudhurst

On top of the world

A spreading horse chestnut in the centre of Goudhurst.

If you want to see glowing vistas across some of the most beautiful rolling countryside in the world, this walk is worth the effort. You'll tackle a few hills, downwards on the outward route and ascending on the way back. It's important not to miss a single thing, so binoculars are a must to enjoy the amazing High Weald of Kent. Goudhurst itself is a delight to explore, with its old weavers' cottages, its oast-house and its village pond with ducks galore.

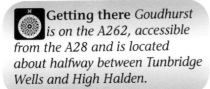 **Getting there** *Goudhurst is on the A262, accessible from the A28 and is located about halfway between Tunbridge Wells and High Halden.*

Length of walk 1 mile.
Time 45 minutes to 1¼ hours.
Terrain Moderately hilly but comfortable underfoot. Some stiles. Unsuitable for buggies.
Start/parking There's a free car park close to the High Street in Balcombes Hill (the B2079). This is the turning opposite the oast-house. Balcombes Hill runs alongside the village pond (GR 722376).
Map OS Explorer 136.
Refreshments The Vine, at the junction of High Street and North Road in Goudhurst, is a child-friendly pub, with the youngsters' own menu. Telephone: 01580 211261.

The Walk

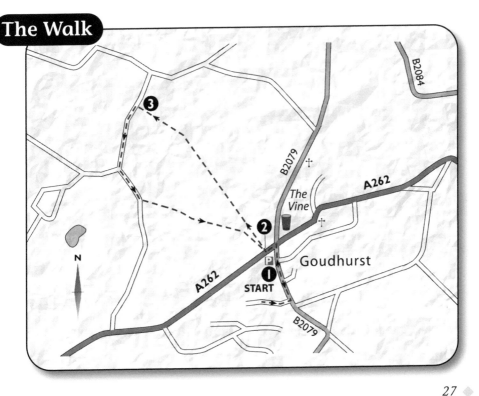

Kiddiwalks in Kent

❶ Turn left out of the car park and walk towards the village pond on your left. Cross West Road carefully and take the footpath opposite, passing the oast-house on your left. Go through the wooden kissing gate ahead, then between a wall and a fence into a meadow. From this point there are stunning views across the High Weald.

❷ Immediately, bear right, downhill along a footpath. Climb a waymarked stile on your right and cross a plank bridge. Follow the footpath ahead to climb another stile and cross another plank bridge. Follow this slightly descending footpath, keeping the tree line to your right. Climb a stile ahead and cross a third plank bridge. Continue with trees on your right and a fenced field on your left. Shortly, climb two stiles close together and follow the path ahead for a short distance, bearing right across a bridge. Climb a stile into a lane and turn left.

❸ Walk along this quiet lane, watching for occasional traffic. After about 300 yards at a fork, take the left lane. Almost immediately, bear left at a public footpath signpost and follow the path uphill through woods. Pass through a kissing gate adjacent to a metal farm gate and follow the winding footpath uphill through meadows towards buildings. When you reach the top of the hill, you'll see the path by the oast-house where you started. Descend, approaching the oast-house, and retrace your steps along the path back to the road.

◆ Fun Things to See and Do ◆

If you take some bread along with you, you could feed the ducks on the lovely village pond at the start of the walk. They are sure to be grateful!

The tower of Goudhurst's village church of St Mary is open to visitors during the summer months and you can climb to the top to see more amazing views of the surrounding countryside.

Goudhurst's village pond.

◆ Background Notes ◆

During the 1700s much of Kent was lawless and at the mercy of criminals and smugglers like the notorious Hawkhurst gang. One of Goudhurst's proudest moments must be when it formed a militia in 1747 to drive the Hawkhurst gang from the village.

Goudhurst also has a long history of farming, as well as weaving, which was brought to the area by Flemish weavers. Look out for the Weavers' Cottages in the village dating from around 1350. During the late-15th to early-17th centuries, Goudhurst also had a number of iron foundries, one of which was used for the manufacture of cannon used against the Spanish Armada in 1588.

6

Cranbrook

A capital visit

The path through Angley Wood.

Cranbrook's title is the 'capital of the Weald of Kent'. Just a short way from the village you can get back to nature wandering through Angley Wood. If possible, visit during May when the woods are carpeted in rolling swathes of bluebells. The walk passes through lovely woodland, pine forests and scrubland, so there are lots of other wildflowers and birds to see. Look out, too, for rabbits scurrying along the ground and grey squirrels leaping from tree to tree. After your walk, you could visit the world famous Sissinghurst Castle Garden which is only a couple of miles away.

Cranbrook

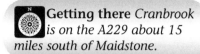

Getting there *Cranbrook is on the A229 about 15 miles south of Maidstone.*

Length of walk 1¾ miles.
Time 1½ hours.
Terrain Comfortable walking but some uneven footpaths so unsuitable for buggies.
Start/parking You can park near the start of the walk in Angley Road, on the A229. Access to the woods is opposite New Road (GR 768359).

Map OS Explorer 136.
Refreshments There is no picnic area so snacks would have to be consumed safari-style. Alternatively, why not visit the Crown pub in Cranbrook High Street for a meal after your walk? The Crown is a family pub, with a garden, and they offer a reasonably priced menu, as well as bar snacks. Telephone: 01580 712089.

The Walk

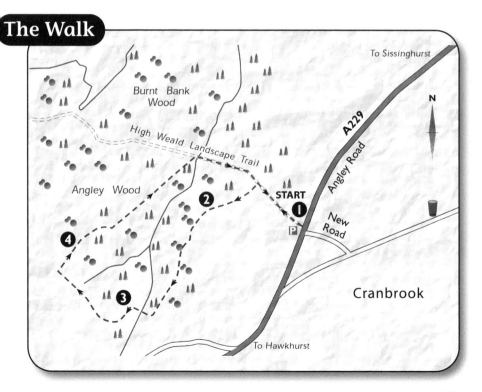

Kiddiwalks in Kent

1 Find the woodland entrance opposite New Road on the eastern side of the A229. Go through the barrier beside a gate, along a wide track. Pass through a gap beside a wooden gate ahead and walk downhill. Shortly, bear left at a High Weald Landscape Trail signpost into woods. Follow the curving path. On reaching an intersecting, wider path, turn left, waymarked.

2 You'll see Goddard's Green through trees on your left as you follow this wider descending path. At a High Weald Landscape Trail signpost, bear left into woods. Shortly, at a signpost, bear right. Soon, go down a dip and beneath pylon wires. As the tree line thins out, ignore a wooden gate into a meadow on your left. Keep following this curving woodland path with tree-fringed meadows to your left and a downhill slope to your right. The path descends sharply to a plank bridge over a brook. Descend four steps and cross the bridge, continuing ahead uphill and then bear left following the waymarker.

3 Follow this narrow track through a clearing. You can see a deeply-pitched house and farm buildings through trees on your left. The footpath makes an abrupt right curve and continues in the same direction. Soon you will see a minor entrance to the woods through a gap beside a wooden gate on the left. Turn right along a wide footpath and walk about 100 yards to take the right fork of a wide track crossing the footpath. Ignore a narrow footpath immediately on the right.

4 This major track is as wide as a conventional road. Keep ahead,

---

◆ Fun Things to See and Do ◆

Take along a wildflower identification book and see if you can name some of the flowers on the woodland floor. When you get home, you could paint or crayon a picture of your favourite flowers.

Bluebell time in the woods.

ignoring left and right turns. The track curves, descends and ascends. Eventually the wide path narrows. Turn right when you reach a major pebbled intersecting track. This track leads you back to the entrance to Angley Wood. Go through the gap beside the wooden gate and metal barrier back to Angley Road.

◆ Background Notes ◆

Cranbrook means a brook where cranes or herons live. Cran Brook eventually became known as the river Crane. During Roman times, iron ore was extracted from local quarries and ironworking was an important industry. Later, because of the many streams running through the area, mills were built from the abundant oak trees and Cranbrook became famous for smooth, woollen cloth, called 'broadcloth'. The medieval village of Cranbrook, with its white, weatherboarded houses, dates from the 11th century.

Located on the A262, two miles north-east of Cranbrook is **Sissinghurst Castle Garden** created by Vita Sackville-West and her husband Sir Harold Nicolson. There is a licensed restaurant and light refreshments are available. No pushchairs are admitted as the paths are uneven, but they will lend you a baby sling or a hip-carrying infant seat. Telephone 01580 710700 for details.

7

Riverside Country Park

Horrid Hill and its horrible hulks

The Medway estuary.

This is a charming walk, full of interest and surprise. Riverside Country Park is situated alongside the Medway estuary and offers a wide variety of habitats for wildlife – mudflats, salt marsh, ponds, reed beds, grassland and scrub. Brent geese and wigeon visit from the Arctic Circle and you may see shore crabs scrabbling among the boulders for food. Fish, such as bass, come to the estuary to spawn, but I think the nicest animals here are the small wild rabbits, so look out for them.

Your walk will take you past Sharp's Green Wildlife Pond, home to small animals like bats and swallows who like to hunt here. In the summer, dragonflies and damselflies hover over the water and there are frogs, newts, sticklebacks and pond-skaters. You will also skirt Eastcourt Meadows, an area rich in wildflowers, trees and shrubs where small mammals live amongst the long grasses.

Riverside Country Park

 Getting there *Rainham is accessible from Junction 4 of the M2. Take the A278 to Gillingham, turn left on the A2 then right on the A289. Riverside Country Park is clearly signposted off Lower Rainham Road, the B2004.*

Length of walk 1½ miles plus an extra ¾ mile if you include Horrid Hill.
Time 45 minutes for the Eastcourt Meadows circular; an extra 30 minutes for Horrid Hill.

(Horrid Hill is linear, except for a loop at the end.)
Terrain Easy, flat walking. Comfortable for pushchairs and buggies up Horrid Hill, but they are not recommended for the main walk around Eastcourt Meadows.
Start/parking Riverside Country Park Visitor Centre (GR 807683).
Map OS Explorer 148.
Refreshments You can enjoy a picnic in one of the designated picnic areas or eat at the visitor centre café.

The Walk

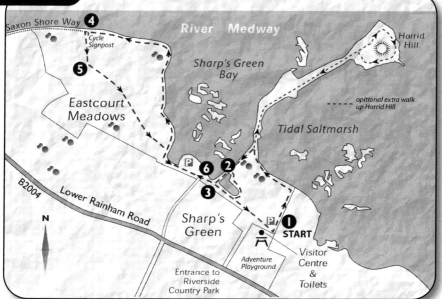

35

Kiddiwalks in Kent

7

① Walk towards the estuary from the rear of the car park, going over a slight incline, and turning left along the riverside path. At an intersection of three paths, bear right towards Horrid Hill for a short distance, then left along the narrow footpath. Follow the footpath through trees. You can still see the salt marshes of the estuary through the trees on your right. Soon you will see a signpost pointing left to Sharp's Green Wildlife Pond.

② Turn left, down steps, to access the fenced boardwalk. Follow the boardwalk all the way looking out for birds, dragonflies and other wild creatures. At the end of the journey around the pond, exit onto a track, turning right to rejoin the estuary path you were on originally.

③ Turn left onto the estuary path, following it until you see a small car park/viewing area ahead of you. Go through a wooden gate, passing the car park, and following the path as it bears right, still keeping close to the estuary. Interesting houseboats and tugs are moored nearby with lovely views over the water. Keep to this path. Soon a bridleway runs to your left behind fences. Shortly, ignore a short wooden waymarker post across the bridleway. Instead, continue ahead, passing, on your right, some cylindrical concrete blocks protecting the riverbank.

④ When you reach a tall blue signpost for cyclists, ignore its directions and turn left. Looking out for horses, pass through a wide gap in the fence, cross the

◆ Fun Things to See and Do ◆

 There are plenty of wide open spaces in Riverside Country Park, just right for a spot of kite flying if there's a nice breeze on the day you visit. At the visitor centre there's an adventure playground for the children as well as conventional swings; whilst inside the centre there is a room set aside with equipment for interactive learning about local wildlife.

The adventure playground near the visitor centre.

bridleway and go through a narrow opening opposite. Continue ahead along a wide grassy marked footpath ignoring a small narrow path to your left.

5 When you reach a fork in the wide path, take the narrower, left-hand track for your return journey. Keep to the track, through widely-spaced hawthorn trees. Go along the path until you reach a thicker copse of trees ahead and take the path through the middle. Now a wire fence enclosing a conservation area runs to your left. Soon, pass through a gap between wooden fences into a triangular clearing, which is part of the bridleway. Watching for horses, walk the short distance to the apex of the clearing and pass through the gap in the fence. You will see the car park/viewing area ahead of you.

Kiddiwalks in Kent

7

6 Go through the gate on the far side of the car park and continue ahead. At a fork in the tracks, decide whether you want to take the shorter route back to the starting point or if you prefer to walk to the end of Horrid Hill.

For the shorter route: Take the right fork and pass the place where you left Sharp's Green Wildlife Pond on your left. Go through the gap ahead between wooden posts, and watching for traffic, turn left into the car park.

For the longer route to Horrid Hill: Take the left fork which gradually curves to the end of Horrid Hill and around a small loop. There is an information board where you can identify landmarks across the river as well as local wildlife. Return to the beginning of Horrid Hill and retrace your steps back to the car park.

◆ Background Notes ◆

Some claim that the long, thin promontory known as Horrid Hill gets its name from the French prisoners who were kept in dreadful conditions in prison ships or 'hulks' moored here during the Napoleonic wars. Charles Dickens wrote about the terrible hulks in his novel *Great Expectations*. Other people claim that there was once a tanning works here, which gave off a horrible smell. In 1902, a cement works was built here. Today, Horrid Hill is a fine place to explore and if you walk right to the end, you can enjoy wonderful views over the estuary and watch the wading birds and gulls, so binoculars are a must. The best time to do this is two hours before high tide.

The bay to your left between Horrid Hill and Eastcourt Meadows is Sharp's Green Bay.

8

Egerton
Roaming the Greensand Ridge

The charming village of Egerton.

I once visited the delightful village of Egerton when the World Cup was in full flow and the tall tower of the ancient ragstone church of St James was flying England's flag. I'm sure God would have approved!

The village itself is quaint and colourful. This lovely walk across the neighbouring countryside is more suited to children old enough to cope with a little rough ground, some stiles and a few, fairly gentle hills. This terrain, of course, affords some fine views, taking in woodlands, fields, meadows and orchards – a walk of much variety. Enjoy it.

8

Getting there *Egerton is south of the M20 approximately halfway between Junctions 8 and 9. If you approach by the A20 there is a bridge over the motorway accessible from near Charing. Well-signposted from neighbouring villages.*

Length of walk 1¾ miles.
Time 1½ hours.
Terrain A challenging circuit, suitable for older children who

have a little more experience of walking. A few stiles and some uneven footpaths.
Start/parking Street parking is available in the little village of Egerton, near the George public house (GR 907475).
Map OS Explorer 137.
Refreshments The George in Egerton is a popular village local that offers a warm welcome to children and has a large outdoor play area. Telephone: 01233 7756304.

The Walk

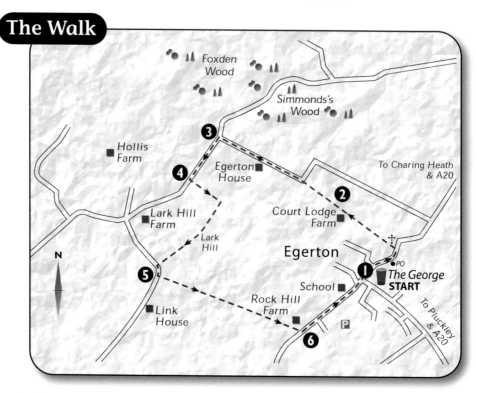

Egerton

1 With the George pub behind you turn right along Stonebridge Green Lane. Shortly, a signpost for the Greensand Way directs you through iron church gates opposite. Bear left around the church and go to the bottom of the churchyard to a waymarked gate in the corner. Go through the gate and continue ahead through an orchard. Keep roughly ahead, skirting orchard tree lines where necessary. When you reach a wood facing you, bear right, following its curving edge and keeping it on your left.

2 Go through a metal farm gate, passing a waymarker post on your left. Continue ahead along a wide, tree-lined track.

Walk through a gap by a metal gate. Shortly pass old cottages on your left and go through a gap beside a wooden gate, passing more buildings. Continue ahead then turn left into a quiet, country lane, Egerton House Road.

3 Pass a large white building on your left, Egerton House. You can walk on a grass verge most of the way. Pass a sign on your left saying 'Egerton House Woods Private' and then, almost immediately, take a footpath left, waymarked, although the signpost may be obscured by trees.

4 Continue with Egerton House

◆ Fun Things to See and Do ◆

While walking, why not collect interesting items for a table decoration? All you will need to complete your decoration at home is a small wicker basket, cheap to buy if you don't already have one. You will find plenty of fascinating items lying on the ground to include in your decoration, like interestingly-shaped twigs, pieces of wood, unusual stones, attractive leaves, acorns or pine cones, according to the season. Later, you could insert some evergreen or coloured leaves, berries or catkins from your own garden and, if you want to make your creation really special, use a gold or silver spray to make your display sparkle.

Woods on your left and a field on your right. At the corner of the woods, turn right along a footpath through the field. On reaching a fence facing you, find a waymarker on a large corner-post. Follow it to the right along a short, narrow footpath, cutting off the corner of the field. At the end, descend five steps through the trees, continuing along a leafy path onto a lane. Turn left.

5 Ignore the first public footpath signpost left – this is blocked by secured farm gates and buildings. Continue ahead along the lane till you reach a wide wooden gate on your left to another footpath. This is not waymarked but is signed 'Please Close This Gate'. Pass through the gate, closing it carefully, and continue by bearing right and hugging the tree line on your

right. Ignore the first opening into an adjacent field. Pass between wooden gate posts ahead (the gate is missing). The field ahead is fenced. Bear right along a short track into an adjacent field, continuing in the same direction, but now with the tree line on your left. At the next corner, climb a stile on your left and go ahead. Now pass between old wooden posts towards a weeping willow tree in the next meadow. Climb a stile in the opposite hedgerow and go ahead to another stile. Climb this stile with care as it's poorly maintained, and then turn left into a lane.

6 Walk a short distance along this lane, gently ascending and watching for traffic. You can use verges part of the way until you reach the proper footpath. Soon you'll see the George pub ahead of you.

◆ Background Notes ◆

The village of Egerton was originally situated on a Roman road from Lympne and stands on the crest of the Greensand Hills known as the Greensand Ridge, marking the northern boundary of the Weald of Kent. Due to the farming tradition which required homesteads to be built adjacent to the land, the homes of Egerton are scattered, some of them some distance away from the lovely old church of St James, parts of which date back to the 13th century.

Warren Street

Look up and down and all around

The footpath to the woods.

This is a picturesque walk through unspoilt countryside, taking in the lovely meadows, farmland and woodlands of Kent's North Downs. The first part of the walk is through open agricultural land and, if you are lucky, you may see hares racing across the fields or some colourful pheasants. The latter part of the walk is partly through woodlands, studded with a variety of wildflowers. In spring or early summer, there are bluebells and primroses, even delicate celandines peeping like little stars from the undergrowth, so don't forget to look down as well as all around you. This is a chance to get away from all the hurly-burly of everyday life and appreciate the tranquillity of an English country walk.

Kiddiwalks in Kent

9

Getting there *From the M20, take Junction 8 and follow signs for the A20 towards Lenham. A short way past Lenham village, turn left into Hubbards Hill and follow the signpost to Warren Street.*

Length of walk 2½ miles.
Time 2 to 2½ hours.
Terrain Mostly flat, with one or two small inclines, several stiles and some walking on rough ground so more suitable for older children. There are short distances to walk along quiet country roads, so watch for occasional traffic.

Start/parking Warren Street, Lenham, near Maidstone. The walk starts near the Harrow Hill Hotel at the top of Hubbards Hill and customers can use their car park whilst doing the walk (GR 927529).
Map OS Explorer 137.
Refreshments There is no official picnic site on the route but there are some good places to stop for a rest or you can eat at the welcoming Harrow Hill Hotel, which has a garden and an outdoor play area. Telephone: 01622 858727.

◆ Fun Things to See and Do ◆

At the end of this walk, you pass through woodlands and if you choose bluebell time, you won't be disappointed by the display. Wildflowers seem to thrive in these woodlands and it might be a good idea for the children to take along an identification book so they can see how many different kinds of plants there are. Also, they can watch out for hares, as well as pheasants, which are easily startled from their hiding places in the undergrowth.

The Walk

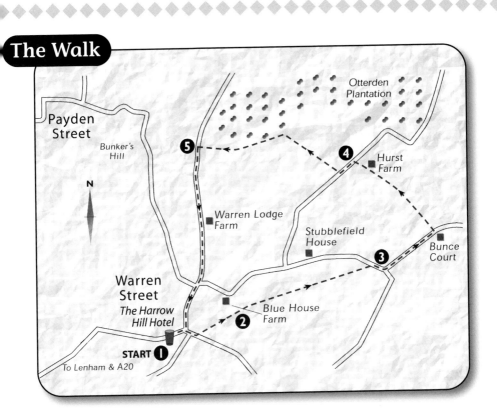

1 From the Harrow Hill Hotel, turn right, then right again down Waterditch Road. Ignore a turning right into Rayners Hill. Climb a stile to your left, waymarked through a field, aiming for a stile in the middle of the facing hedgerow. Climb the stile.

2 Cross this field, aiming for a large tree by a metal gate. Climb the adjacent stile. Follow the designated footpath across the field, in line with the stile step. You'll see a large house ahead. Walk diagonally right towards an outcrop of trees. At the bottom of the outcrop of trees, a corner-post is waymarked ahead. Follow this waymark, passing under the pylon wires. Go towards a metal gate ahead and climb the adjacent stile into a lane, turning right.

3 Follow this lane, soon curving left, with houses and meadows on your right. Shortly, on reaching 'Bunce Court' on your right (see *Background Notes*), follow the green public footpath signpost to the left. This is pheasant and hare country, so watch out for them. Follow the line of pylons then climb the stile ahead, passing another wooden pylon on your left. Ascend a small hill, with a copse on your right. Shortly, ignore a stile on your right, and continue ahead towards farm buildings. Go through the metal gate, waymarked, into Hurst Farm, then exit to Hurstwood Road. This is a quiet country lane, but be aware of occasional traffic.

4 After about 50 yards, climb a stile on your right and go across a field towards woodlands. At the facing tree line, bear gently left, then sharp right into the woods and along a little track for a few yards. At a wider track crossing your path, turn left. After about 60 yards, turn left along another track, and then, shortly, take the next right turn. Follow this curving woodland track until you reach a fork in the paths. Take the right fork, which soon curves left then right to exit onto Slade Road.

5 Again, this is a quiet road, but watch for traffic. It is about 600 yards to the end, where you bear right to cross the junction with Payden Street and then continue ahead into the village of Warren Street where the hotel is on your left.

◆ Background Notes ◆

The Harrow Hill Hotel was once the Harrow Inn – and before that it was a forge and rest house for travellers to Canterbury along the ancient Pilgrims' Way. The Pilgrims' Way was the route taken by pilgrims from Winchester to the shrine of St Thomas Becket at Canterbury.

On the walk you will pass **Bunce Court**, significant for having been a school for refugee Jewish children from Nazi Germany, at which time it was run by educationalist Miss Anna Essinger.

10
Appledore

Water, water, everywhere nor any drop to drink

The Royal Military Canal at Appledore.

This walk is in two loops, making a rough figure of eight, so you can do one or both. Either way, you'll enjoy the sights and sounds of wild creatures that live along the Royal Military Canal and other little waterways in the area. The Royal Military Canal was built in 1804 as a defence against Napoleon should his army invade Britain. There were cannon strategically placed and a cunning plan to fill the canal with salt so there would be no water for the marauding soldiers to drink. Clever, huh?

Kiddiwalks in Kent

10

Getting there *Appledore is located south of Ashford on the B2080 Tenterden road on the edge of Romney Marsh.*

Length of walk Each loop 1¼ miles, total 2½ miles.
Time First loop: 45 minutes; second loop: 1 hour.
Terrain Fairly easy walking but not recommended for buggies. Care needs to be taken at the end of Loop 1, where the footpath curves downwards near the canal.
Start/parking The Black Lion, The Street, Appledore. Street parking is available, as well as designated car parks along The Street (GR 957293).
Map OS Explorer 125.
Refreshments The Black Lion is open all day, every day, and has a varied menu, with something to suit all tastes. Telephone: 01233 758206.

The Walk

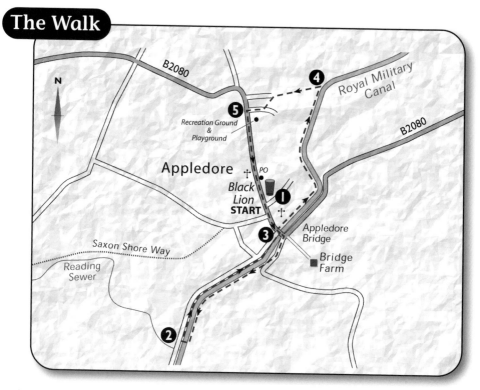

❶ Turn left from the pub and walk downhill along the lane past houses, watching for traffic. Cross the bridge to the far side of the canal and turn right along a tarmac lane, with a private car park to the left. Go through the open gate to take the public footpath along Priory Farm's drive, passing the farm on your left, then pass through a wooden gate, or climb the adjacent stile, and continue along the grassy bank of the canal. When you reach a bridge, go through the gate, turn right over the bridge, then immediately right and through another wooden gate to return along the opposite bank.

❷ Walk back along this narrower, raised footpath, looking down on the canal to your right, with fine views over the farmland to your left. At the end of the footpath, take care as there is a slope to the downhill path for a short distance. Aim for the wooden gate ahead and go through onto the road, watching for traffic.

◆ Fun Things to See and Do ◆

Watch out for the kingfisher, although sometimes all you see is a flash of orange and blue; the mute swan with its s-shaped neck and orange bill; and in summer the amazing, iridescent emperor dragonfly.

Listen out for the marsh frog, who was introduced to the area in the 1930s from Hungary. He might be heard making a loud laughing noise – although he has no reason to laugh because he is the grey heron's favourite dinner!

You could also have some fun playing pooh sticks from one of the bridges on the walk. Everyone enjoys finding a twig and throwing it into the water and then rushing to the other side of the bridge to see it float past.

Sheep looking for a cool spot by the water.

❸ Cross the road carefully and go through a gate almost opposite, beside a nature information board, to follow a lovely stretch of the Royal Military Canal, still on your right. Another stream runs to your left and you are walking along a wide grassy track between the two waterways. Follow the bank as it curves left, with a farm on your left and go through a wooden kissing gate ahead. There are houses in the middle distance on your left. Soon, pass a wooden post telling you it is 13 miles to Hythe. Shortly, climb a stile on your left behind a National Trust post.

❹ Now a stream runs to your right. Continue straight ahead, along a raised ridge, towards houses. Sheep occasionally wander along this ridge, so you may have to slow down! At the end of the ridge, go through a gap just left of the stile ahead. Cross the next field diagonally left, continuing in the same direction along an access road to a pumping station. With the pumping station behind you, follow the road past houses on your right. To your left, just before you reach the main road, is a playing field with an adventure playground, so you may want to stop and try out the equipment.

5 Turn left along the road, crossing to use the wider footpath on the opposite side. Pass Magpie Farm on your right, then the post office on your left. Before you return to your car, look out for the lovely old church of St Peter and St Paul as it's very close to the pub and well worth a visit.

◆ Background Notes ◆

The Royal Military Canal was built as part of England's defences against Napoleon in the early 19th century. It dates from 1804 and was re-fortified when Hitler was in power. It runs for 28 miles from Hythe in the north-east of Romney Marsh to Cliff End in the south-west. It cost £234,000 to build, which is about £10 million in today's money.

Appledore was part of the Peasants' Revolt in 1381 when Hornes Place, which is just outside the village, was sacked by Wat Tyler's men. Jack Cade, another Kent hero who fought for justice, marched through The Street in 1450 and many Appledore men joined him. Some of the lovely houses date from that time.

Where the **Black Lion** pub stands today, there was once a market and a fair authorised by King Edward III. This was held until the end of the 1900s.

11
Great Chart

The Stour Valley Special and Commando Kid Extra

Taking a break by the river.

The Stour Valley walk is one of the most delightful in the book, with rolling meadows of grazing sheep and cattle, lashings of wildflowers, sparkling waterways, and ancient spreading trees. For part of the walk, you will retrace your steps. This is for your safety, to avoid using an unmanned railway crossing and a rickety bridge over the Great Stour. However, I promise it will be wonderful to enjoy the marvellous scenery again from the opposite direction!

The Commando Kid Extra is a very short additional circuit giving you the opportunity to see the delightful variety of old buildings along The Street. Then you can walk through a short stretch of pleasant, newly-created woodland to the extra circuit's main attraction, a state-of-the-art adventure playground.

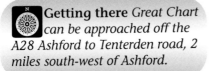

Getting there *Great Chart can be approached off the A28 Ashford to Tenterden road, 2 miles south-west of Ashford.*

Length of walk Stour Valley Special 3 miles. Commando Kid Extra 1 mile.

Time 2–3 hours (plus 30 – 45 minutes for the Commando Kid Extra).

Terrain Easy walking, with a number of stiles on the main Stour Valley walk. Neither walk is suitable for buggies although access to the adventure playground via Singleton Road is fine.

Start/parking The Swan pub, The Street, Great Chart. No parking is available at the pub but plenty on street (GR 981421).

Map OS Explorer 137.

Refreshments The Swan is a 16th-century building that offers a warm welcome and good food. Telephone: 01233 623250.

The Walk

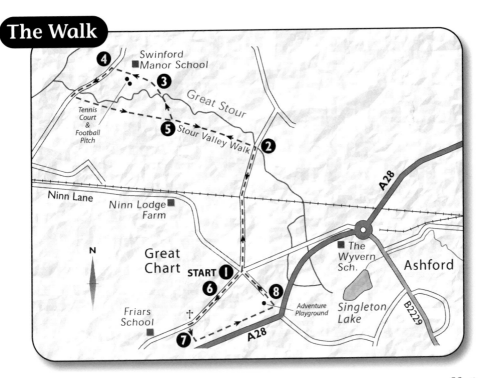

1 Turn left from the Swan, carefully cross Ninn Lane and turn left along a single track lane, waymarked, passing a playing field and a cricket pavilion on your right. Go ahead on a track through farmland and shortly pass through a black metal gate to cross the railway bridge, waymarked. Continue ahead through lovely meadows and, on reaching a metal farm gate, go through the small kissing gate to its left, continuing in the same direction, approaching the Great Stour. Just before the bridge, climb the stile on your left.

2 The footpath bears left curving away from the Great Stour. Soon, turn left across a plank bridge, waymarked, and turn right, with a tree line to your right. Climb the stile ahead into the next field. Cross the field, aiming for the metal gate and adjacent stile opposite and climb the stile. Cross this field towards a bridge over the Great Stour and walk over the bridge.

3 Aim for another metal gate ahead and climb the adjacent stile. Continue, with a waterway running on your left. As the waterway curves away left, continue ahead with wire fencing and a tree line to your left. The next stile is in the facing tree line. Climb this stile and cross a plank bridge over a ditch, then immediately climb the opposite stile. Walk towards another tree line facing you and cross two stiles close together between the

◆ Fun Things to See and Do ◆

The magnificent adventure playground on the optional extra circuit caters for all energetic kids, from little ones who are happy with their rockers, swings and slides, to the older children who long to play real adventure games on the assortment of frames, ramps, swinging tyres and other inventive apparatus. If the kids want even more fun, why not take a football along and practise a little in the open space near the playground? All England players have to start somewhere, after all.

Burning off energy on the Commando Course.

trees, continuing ahead past a tennis court and football pitch.

4 Go through a kissing gate into a lane and, watching for traffic, turn left. Go over a bridge and, almost immediately, turn left at a public footpath signpost. Go straight ahead, aiming for a gap in the tree line ahead, into the next field. Aim for a stile ahead and climb the stile. Follow a line of wooden pylons to climb the next stile, and then continue following the pylons to climb another stile.

5 Now you are retracing your steps. Continue along a tree line and turn left over the plank bridge, then right, following the pylons. Climb a stile and go right. Continue through the kissing gate right of the metal farm gate. Follow the track back to The Street, carefully crossing Ninn Lane as you approach the pub on your right.

The Commando Kid Extra:

6 Pass the pub, continuing along The Street, past lovely old cottages. Look out for an almshouse and then the Old School House, both on your left. On reaching the church of St Mary the Virgin on your right, turn left, waymarked, along Hillcrest. At the green public footpath sign, turn left in front of houses, shortly bearing right with garages to your left. Go left through a waymarked kissing gate ahead.

7 Bear left along a grassy footpath with views of Ashford ahead, descending through young trees. Pass through a wooden gate at the end of the path and walk alongside a meadow with woods on your left. In the far corner of the meadow is the adventure playground, with conventional swings, slides and rocking horses for the little ones and an assortment of excellent climbing frames, ramps and rubber tyres – a great place to play commandos!

8 After enjoying the playground, go through the gate onto Singleton Road, turning left. At the end turn left into The Street.

◆ Background Notes ◆

Great Chart dates back around 1,200 years and is mentioned in many ancient documents. About 1,100 years ago it was sacked by the Danes and before that, in AD 776, its manor, villages and lands were sold to the Archbishop of Canterbury to enable King Egbert of Kent to fight the powerful King Offa of Mercia who had pronounced himself king of all the English. There was a great battle at Otford and it's claimed a red cross appeared in the sky.

The Perpendicular **church of St Mary**, passed on the shorter circuit, is a particularly fine building, with medieval windows. In front of it is the 15th-century timber-framed **Pest House**. A pest house was a hospital for plague victims or those suffering from infectious illnesses.

12

Harty Ferry, Isle of Sheppey

A little island paradise

The paddock near the start of the walk.

This part of Sheppey is unspoilt in the best sense of the word. Birds of prey like kestrels and harriers hover overhead searching for their dinner and, as you drive along Harty Ferry Road on your way to the Ferry House Inn, you will need to stop for the occasional pheasant or pair of grouse who take their time crossing the road. This is their country and they know it – so you just have to be patient and let them pass because they refuse to be hurried! Of course, this gives you a good opportunity to appreciate their fine plumage.

The open fields are home to the hare and the rabbit. On your return journey, you will pass a large, tranquil, tree-fringed lake, which teems with ducks and geese, while hedgerows everywhere are alive with the chirping of small songbirds.

Getting there *From the M2, take the Sittingbourne exit (Junction 5). Head north along the A249 towards Sheerness and cross Kings Ferry Bridge. Follow signs to Leysdown and look for Harty Ferry, signposted to the right. The Ferry House Inn is about 4 miles down Harty Ferry Road.*

Length of walk 2½ miles.
Time 1½ to 2 hours.

Terrain Comfortable walking on wide tracks, partly flat and partly hilly. Not suitable for buggies or pushchairs.
Start/parking The Ferry House Inn, which has a large car park (GR 014659).
Map OS Explorer 149.
Refreshments The Ferry House Inn where children's portions are available. It also has a play area outside for younger children, with swings and novelty rides. Telephone: 01795 510214.

The Walk

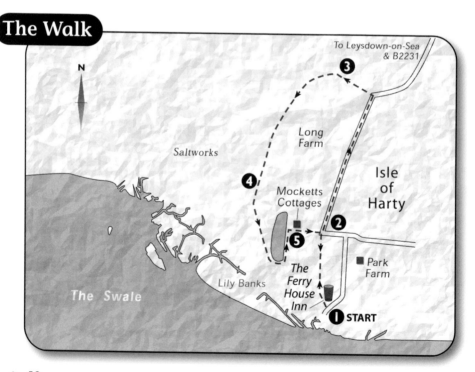

Harty Ferry, Isle of Sheppey

1 Go to the bottom of the Ferry House Inn car park towards the estuary. Turn right and go through a gap by a metal gate, passing a clay pigeon shooting area. Just before the bend curves left towards the estuary, turn right through a wooden gate, waymarked by a blue arrow and go diagonally left across a small orchard. Go through another gate, again waymarked diagonally left, and through a paddock to pass through another gate into a field. (Don't forget to shut the gates securely to keep the ponies safe.) Follow the waymark straight ahead along the edge of a field, with a hedgerow to your right.

2 Cross a concrete intersecting path waymarked ahead, passing a farm on your left and continuing through agricultural land. Keep to the path, with the hedgerow on your right. On reaching another intersecting track, turn left, continuing between open fields. You are now skirting a very large field.

3 As the track curves left, ignore another track to your right. Pass a dyke running at right-angles from the track on your right-hand side. Continue along the main track which changes to grass, with a dyke running alongside on your right. Soon, ignore and pass a gate into a field on your right. Keep following the track curving around the large field on your left, ignoring a track turning left towards a facing row of trees. Start ascending, still curving left. Soon you will be on a ridge. Continue in the same direction. If

◆ Fun Things to See and Do ◆

This really is an excellent opportunity for birdwatching. Why not take along your bird identification book and notepad, as well as a pair of binoculars? The children could have a friendly competition to see who can spot the most species of birds. Don't forget to look upwards as well as around you, as it would be a pity to miss the magnificent birds of prey which are so much a part of Sheppey's magic.

you look back, the ridge extends behind you in a straight line across the fields.

4 Now there are wooden posts on the right and the estuary is in view, also to your right. Soon you will pass a beautiful large lake on your left, teeming with wildfowl. Pass a high wire fence on your right and keep bearing left, following the tree line around the lake. Ahead is a white house and, to its right, the farm you saw on your outward journey. The Ferry House Inn can be seen ahead, further to the right, near the estuary.

5 Turn right along a track, passing in front of the white house. When you reach the farm,

The view from the pub's garden.

turn right along the concrete track crossing your path, towards the estuary. Continue on as it curves to the left. Follow the bridleway sign to the right. Hug the hedgerow to your left, retracing your steps through the gate ahead, crossing the paddock diagonally left to pass through the gate. Cross the orchard and go through the gate, turning left back towards the pub.

◆ Background Notes ◆

The **Isle of Sheppey's** name is derived from the Saxon word *sceapige* which means 'island of sheep'. The island, with a population of around 38,000, measures 9 miles by 4 miles, a large part of which is marshy and is used for grazing sheep.

The **Ferry House Inn** dates from the 16th century and its name is taken from the ferry that once operated between the island and Faversham. Oyster smacks were used in the 19th century to ferry passengers, who had to help with loading and unloading. If there was no wind, the ferry had to be rowed across.

13
Dungeness

Smugglers, a spook and an upside-down schooner

The beach at Dungeness (courtesy of P. Howdle).

This walk is most suitable for older children and has been chosen for its many points of historical interest. The children can climb to the top of one of the lighthouses and enjoy panoramic views over Romney Marsh; they can see Dungeness's magnificent lifeboat close-up; and they can imagine how smugglers practised their illegal trade at dead of night on the wide shingle beaches still dotted with ancient winches. They will also see a pub, called the Pilot, which started out as an upside-down boat and is claimed to be haunted by the Grey Lady reputed to have been a passenger deliberately shipwrecked by Dungeness's fearsome 'wreckers'. And if this is not enough, the Light Railway Café serves the crispiest, most lipsmacking chips!

Kiddiwalks in Kent

13

Getting there *From the A259 (Romney Road), take the B2075 towards Lydd airport to access Dungeness Road. The café and car park are at the end of Dungeness Road.*

Length of walk 2 miles.
Time 1 to 2 hours, although it may be longer if you visit the sites on the way.
Terrain Mostly shingle and rough grass, fairly flat, with a few shingle dunes. Not recommended for buggies.

Start/parking The large car park by the Light Railway Café (GR 088169).
Map OS Explorer 125.
Refreshments The Light Railway Café serves all-day breakfasts and snacks whenever trains are running. For train timetable, telephone 01797 362353. Alternatively, if you would rather eat halfway along your walk, the Pilot Inn is an excellent child-friendly pub. Telephone: 01797 320314.

The Walk

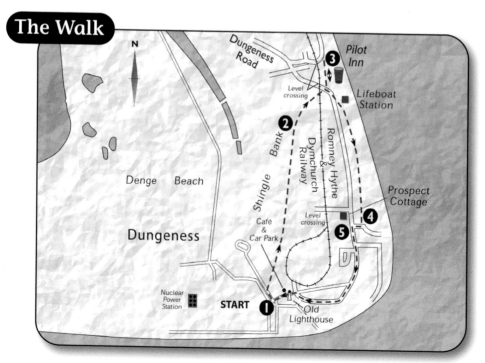

1 You can't miss the old lighthouse just yards from the car park. Now is the time to decide whether you wish to climb its 169 steps to the top for a fine view – or perhaps save it till you return from your walk. Also, impossible to miss, is the enormous nuclear power station which played a vital part in the regeneration of Dungeness by providing an area of shelter from heavy winds. To begin your walk, find two white drums marking the route on the other side of the car park, opposite the lighthouse. Pass between the drums, with the power station on your left and the light railway line to your right. Follow this shingle and grass

◆ Fun Things to See and Do ◆

If you are feeling energetic, you might like to climb the 169 steps up the old Dungeness lighthouse and enjoy panoramic views over Romney Marsh.

Also worth a visit on your walk, is the Dungeness Lifeboat Station. You can see this beautiful vessel free of charge, ready and waiting to be towed by tractor to rescue those in difficulties on the sea and climb the viewing platform to see the radios inside the cabin.

A ride on the Romney Hythe and Dymchurch railway, described as 13½ miles of mainline in miniature, is another treat in store if you have the time. The station is beside the café. Enquire at the booking office for train times, to see how they fit in with your plans for walking and lunch. The times between trains vary from 40 minutes to 1 hour 20 minutes. The stations served are Dungeness, Romney Sands, New Romney, Dymchurch and Hythe. There is a model railway exhibition at New Romney station with over twenty trains, as well as a toy collection, dolls and posters. Telephone: 01797 362353.

track past a thick copse of dwarf broom. Continue and pass to the right of another copse of broom. To the left, a row of large posts runs between the track and power station property. There are many criss-cross paths, so just keep in view a large, white building ahead, with a chimney extending from the left of the roof. Continue until you reach a large, crescent-shaped bank of shingle.

❷ At the shingle bank, bear right, aiming towards light signals at a level crossing beside a bright green building. When you reach the level crossing which bisects the road, cross the road diagonally right with caution, simultaneously passing over the railway line. Go past the green building and you will see ahead the sign for the Pilot Inn. The children will like the wonderful signpost facing you in the pub garden showing directions and distances, not only to Land's End, Calais and Majorca, but also to such exotic places as Kiev, Cairo, Caracas, Lapland and the North Pole.

❸ From the Pilot Inn, go down the concrete track through holiday homes towards the coastline. Turn right and walk on

the grass beside the coast road to visit the lifeboat station and see the Dungeness *Pride and Spirit* lifeboat. It really is something! After admiring the lifeboat, you might like to wander across the beach and see some of the old winches, both metal and wooden, still lying there. Then continue in the same direction, with the coast road on your right.

❹ When you reach an intersecting pathway from the road to the sea, turn right, back to the road. (There is dangerous machinery around the boats ahead and further progress is banned.) As you reach the road, you'll see, facing you slightly to the right, a black cottage with bright yellow window frames. This is Prospect Cottage once owned by the famous film director Derek Jarman, who made the lovely sculptured garden.

❺ Turn left, walking on grass beside the road. Eventually, you will pass a sign saying 'Sleepers Cottages'. Continue ahead, ignoring a right turn along a concrete road, until you reach a black and white banded lighthouse on a concrete plinth on your left. This is Dungeness's working lighthouse. Follow the road as it bears right till you reach your starting point. The old lighthouse will be on your left and the car park and café straight ahead.

◆ Background Notes ◆

Due to its isolation, the area has in the past attracted ruthless smugglers who practised 'wrecking'. Fires were lit on beaches to 'warn' shipping, but these smugglers started the fires in the wrong places, to lure ships aground. As the sea was shallow, people did not drown but were murdered instead for the ship's booty. In 1640, a three-masted schooner foundered on Dungeness beach and the occupants were slaughtered for gold and brandy. This schooner, the *Alfresia*, was turned upside down and holes were cut into it for windows and doors and the original **Pilot Inn** was born. It was replaced in the 1950s by the present-day construction, although this retains some of the character of the original. The Pilot Inn's ghost is claimed to be a lady passenger from the *Alfresia* and she often gives the staff a nasty scare.

The erection of **lighthouses** put an end to the smugglers' activities, but as the sea receded, new lighthouses had to be built. The old lighthouse with the 169 steps was the fourth and dates from 1901. The modern black and white lighthouse dates from 1961.

Sleepers Cottages passed on the route are homes originally made from old railway sleepers, although some people have smartened them up with new fronts. Some of them have been placed two together to make a larger home – the slight arch in the roofs shows their origins. They were built during the 1920s and purchased for about £10 but now they are worth up to £150,000 and it's fun trying to spot which homes originate from railway carriages. These people were responsible for helping regenerate the area.

14

Rough Common

The woods are alive!

Broom covers the common in springtime.

Yes, the woods really are alive – with the sounds of tits, nuthatches, treecreepers and three species of woodpecker. Its sunny glades are home to butterflies, willow warblers and robins, while nightjars visit from Africa in the summer. There are lots of hazel trees and oaks, which provide nuts for the saucy squirrels and little brown dormice. This is a delightful woodland walk which includes heathland, providing the variety of habitats that enrich the natural wildlife.

Getting there *Rough Common Road is off the A290 Canterbury to Whitstable road.*

Length of walk 2 miles.
Time 40 minutes.
Terrain Easy, gently undulating, well-trodden dirt footpaths. Buggies at your discretion, remembering these are natural woodlands and paths can be bumpy.
Start/parking To reach Rough Common car park and picnic area, take the brown sign to Blean Wood Nature Reserve, off Rough Common Road. Turn into Ross Gardens and bear sharp right along a narrow track, signposted. The reserve's car parks are at the end (GR 121593).
Map OS Explorer 150.
Refreshments There are no eating facilities on this route, but nothing can be more pleasant than taking along your own food to eat in the designated picnic area of this idyllic woodland setting. After your walk, you could join the A290 Whitstable Road (exiting left from Rough Common Road) for an easy 20 minute drive to Whitstable, a quaint seaside fishing town. Then get yourself some fish and chips. There are no better fish and chips than those available in Whitstable and that's official!

◆ Fun Things to See and Do ◆

In the summer months, this is a great place to look for ants' nests, often found around rotting tree stumps – sometimes these are colonised by the large, reddish wood ants and they are fascinating to watch as they busy themselves around their nest. Take a magnifying glass so you can see the little creatures scurrying here and there, some carrying nesting material or food for their young. These are the worker ants. The enormous queen, who lays the eggs, is hidden away deep in the nest and hardly moves. She, too, has to be fed and looked after.

◆◆◆**14**◆◆◆◆◆◆◆◆◆◆◆◆◆◆◆◆◆◆◆◆◆◆◆◆◆◆◆◆◆◆◆◆◆◆

The Walk

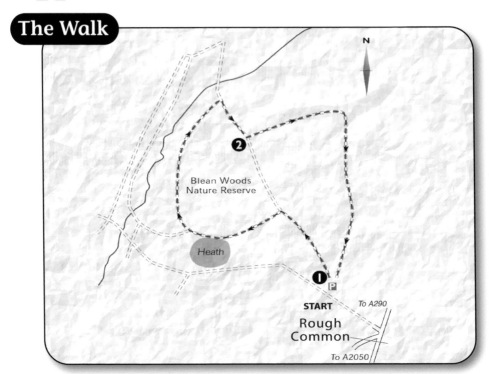

1 Facing the large, main information board in the car park, take the left fork, waymarked, passing with the information board to your right. You are following the green route. Follow the footpath, then cross a narrow intersecting track and bear left at the fork ahead, waymarked. Continue through woods, past a memorial glade for Brian Hawkes, a well-known naturalist (1931–1990). Continue on the footpath, crossing a clearing, curving right into woods.

2 At a narrow intersecting path, go straight ahead, waymarked. At the next signpost, in the centre of the footpath, follow the green arrow along the right fork. Soon, cross an intersecting path, and continue ahead, waymarked, beginning to descend. Cross a small clearing. At the next intersecting path, turn right along a wide, grassy track. Follow this track for a while. When I was here, the birds were making such a din I almost had to cover my ears!

Picnic time on the common.

Eventually, at a T-junction of paths, bear right – in early summer, there may be swathes of star-like wood anemones to be seen. Keep going, following the green arrows ahead, descending. The path gradually begins to ascend. At the end of the footpath, (which converges with another) you will see ahead a green arrow pointing to the right. Follow this gently curving footpath back to the car park.

◆ Background Notes ◆

The nature reserve is jointly owned by Natural England, the Royal Society for the Protection of Birds, the Woodland Trust, Canterbury City Council, Kent County Council and Swale Borough Council and is a Site of Special Scientific Interest.

In days gone by, the ancient forest of Blean was used by royalty for hunting and later became a haunt of smugglers. Once it stretched from the Great Stour to the east of Canterbury, to the coast.

15

Brockhill Country Park

Fantabulous family fun

Enjoying the playground at the start of the route.

There's nothing more relaxing than wandering along a pleasant footpath beside a lazy stream. And if you'd like to stop and watch a gurgling waterfall, then this is the walk for you. The scenery on both walks is picturesque, and the views on the longer stroll are truly breathtaking.

Along the way there are lots of interesting things for children to see, and in spring maybe some lambs skipping in the meadows. There are also rabbits and squirrels but the children have to be quiet and sharp-eyed to spot them.

Brockhill Country Park

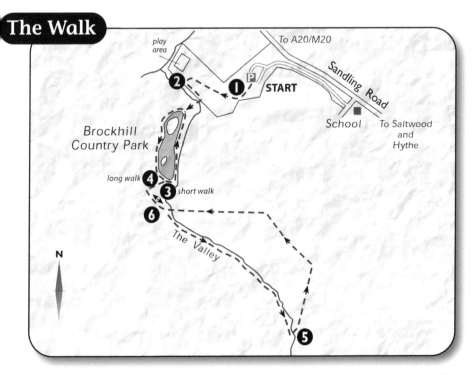

Getting there *Brockhill Country Park is near Hythe, close to the village of Saltwood and Junction 11 of the M20. The park shares an entrance with Brockhill School, situated just ½ mile south of Sandling station.*

Length of walk Lake Walk: ¾ mile; Valley Walk: 1½ miles.
Time Lake Walk – 30 to 45 minutes. Valley Walk – add on 45 minutes to 1 hour.

Terrain The shorter Lake Walk is mostly flat and is ideal for buggies, but the longer Valley Walk is unsuitable, with steps and a few hills to climb.
Start/parking Brockhill Country Park pay and display car park (GR 148359).
Map OS Explorer 138.
Refreshments The visitor centre provides hot and cold food and drinks in a pleasant woodland setting. Picnic areas available. Telephone for further details: 01303 266327.

The Walk

① The visitor centre is next to the car park. Go along the main footpath with the centre on your right, through the picnic area, slightly uphill. The footpath swings right and, at the fork, go ahead to continue your walk, signposted 'Lake' or take the other path to visit the lovely adventure playground.

② Continue along the footpath to the lake, bearing left with woods and a wooden fence to your right, shortly descending. Soon bear sharp right along the path, then left over a wooden bridge crossing Brockhill Stream. Continue ahead, passing a signboard on your right. Bear right, waymarked, and follow the path round the end of the lake, curving to the left over a wooden bridge. Walk along the footpath on the long side of the lake. If you are walking the lake route only, continue to (3) but if you are walking the longer valley route, skip (3) and move on to (4).

③ *Lake Walk only:* Follow the footpath along the far short end of the lake. (Optional: Just before you are about to bear left along the other long side of the lake, find a right turn down steps leading to the waterfall. After seeing the waterfall, rejoin the lakeside path, turning right.) If you do not take the optional peek at the waterfall, simply follow the lakeside path to the left. Turn right at the end of the lake, bearing right over the wooden bridge you used on your outward journey, and retrace your steps back to the visitor centre.

④ *To continue to the Valley Walk from the end of (2):* Ignoring the left bend of the far short end of the lake, follow the path right uphill, then bear left, ignoring and passing a gate and stile on

---

◆ Fun Things to See and Do ◆

You could have a wonderful game playing pooh sticks from one of the little bridges. Try out different lengths and thicknesses of twigs to see which works best.

your right. There are woods to your left and meadows to your right. Soon, go through a gate, bearing right, with a fence and meadow to your right. Keep to this footpath, hugging the fence. You'll see the stream flowing below left. Shortly, pass a wooden gate on your right. Here the stream goes underground for a few yards. Continue with the stream on your left and the fence on your right, over boards where muddy. Follow the path as it bears left, ignoring the sign saying Brockhill Boundary on your right. Go down steps, curving left, cross a wooden bridge, and climb steps the other side.

5 Climb the grassy slope ahead, turning left at the top along the ridge. After passing the large tree in the centre of the meadow, bear left towards the far corner by the stream and cross the wooden bridge. If the stream is full, you could play pooh sticks – if you look around, there are plenty lying on the ground. Then go ahead, through the gate, following the footpath bearing right.

6 Shortly, turn right and descend some steps through the 'wooded dell', along a boardwalk, and then bear right to the waterfall. After enjoying the waterfall, continue in the same direction to rejoin the original footpath around the lake a little further down and turn right. Now the lake is on your left, and the stream is on your right. Turn right at the end of the lake, bearing right over the wooden bridge and retrace your steps back to the visitor centre.

◆ Background Notes ◆

Brockhill Country Park dates back to Norman times and was part of a large estate. The old Jacobean manor house still exists, having been integrated into the buildings of Brockhill School which shares its entrance with the park. The valley formed part of the estate's farmland and Brockhill Stream runs through it towards the Royal Military Canal at Hythe. The waterfall, visited on the return journey, dates from the 1870s, although it has since been rebuilt.

16

Stelling Minnis

A windmill wonderland

On the route near Stelling Minnis.

This is a gentle stroll starting from a friendly pub in this enchanting village setting, taking in a fine old smock windmill, quiet country lanes and beautiful meadows with farm animals, including some very inquisitive horses. The wide, comfortable grassy footpaths are lined with trees and shrubs with plenty of gaps so you can see the splendid views beyond them, while wildflowers grow in abundance in the grass verges and hedgerows.

Getting there *Stelling Minnis is signposted* approximately 7 miles south of Canterbury off the B2068 (Canterbury to Hythe road).

Length of walk 1¾ miles.
Time 45 minutes to 1½ hours.
Terrain Flat, comfortable walking, although the pebbled, occasionally potholed paths are not recommended for buggies and pushchairs.
Start/parking The Rose and Crown, Minnis Lane, Stelling Minnis (GR 141469). The pub has a large car park and there is plenty of street parking.

Map OS Explorer 138.
Refreshments The Rose and Crown in Minnis Lane is an old coaching inn, which offers a friendly welcome to both adults and children. The youngsters can choose from their own menu which includes chicken nuggets and veggie 'teddies', amongst other dishes. Telephone 01227 709265. If you are walking on a Sunday or Bank Holiday, an alternative is to enjoy a cream tea at the windmill which is located halfway along the walk, and you pass it again on the way back. Telephone: 01227 709550/709238.

◆ Fun Things to See and Do ◆

If you are here on a Sunday or Bank Holiday, a visit to Stelling Minnis windmill, which you pass on your walk, is a *must*. The windmill's sails, or blades, are rotated by the wind and this drives a pump or generator which in turn grinds the corn to make bread and cereal. The mill was built in 1866 and it was working until 1970 but now houses a museum telling the story of mills and millers, as well as serving delicious cream teas.

The Walk

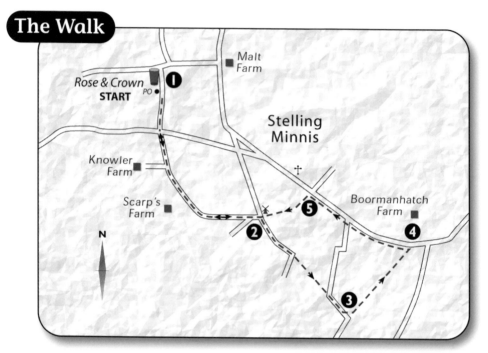

❶ From the Rose and Crown in Minnis Lane, turn right and walk down the wide, grass-verged lane, past the post office and general store on your right. Bearing left, cross the road carefully and enter the lane almost opposite, signed 'Public footpath to Knowler Farm'. Continue through meadows, ignoring a right turn to Knowler Farm, also passing a signpost on the right to Scarp's Farm. Follow a left bend, soon passing between hedges to houses, and then go along a narrow tree-lined footpath onto Mill Lane. Opposite is the windmill.

❷ Turn right along the continuation of Mill Lane, with houses and the mill behind you, and passing a sign on your right saying 'Stelling Minnis Bye Laws'. You will reach a three-pronged intersection: ignore the left (a grass track) and the right (to a house) but take the central main path. At the end bear right between wooden posts along a track towards cottages.

3 Just before the cottages, bear left crossing a green and go past a house with a wooden post box, then turn left, along a lovely tree-lined track. You can see a long ridge behind fields to your right. Soon you will see a white house in its own grounds on your left. Its grounds extend as far as the footpath you are walking, but the house is set well back. Turn left around the grounds.

4 Continue along this pleasant track until you reach a red-brick house on your right. Bear left to follow the high hedge curving around the white house already mentioned. Follow the track, cross a concrete lane and go ahead along a narrower track with hedges on your left and

trees to your right towards a red-brick house. Turn right in front of the house and go between trees to open ground with copses, following two small curves in the path bearing right. Almost immediately, the windmill will come into view. Now turn right along a short, straight track and the windmill is ahead, slightly left.

5 Take the left footpath towards the windmill, passing Old Mill House and a single-storey workshop on your right. Pass the windmill on your right. Rejoin the path you arrived on, through the tunnel of trees opposite, set slightly right, and retrace your steps to the start.

◆ Background Notes ◆

'Stelling' is derived from the Latin for 'cattle shelter'. Stelling Minnis was originally a small trading hamlet and most of the old village, which occupied the site of the church of St Mary the Virgin, was wiped out when the Black Death swept through the area. The local people redeveloped their village around The Minnis.

The **mill** was built by two brothers called Holman in 1866 and is now owned by Kent County Council and managed by Stelling Minnis Borough Council. It remained a working mill until the last miller, Alec Davison, died in 1970. It was eventually renovated at a cost of £120,000 and is now a Grade I listed building.

17

Upstreet, Grove Ferry

Stomping through Stodmarsh

One of the wide tracks through the nature reserve.

This lovely country walk takes in the Saxon Shore Way and the Stour Valley Walk through an unspoilt area criss-crossed with delightful waterways, farmland and meadows of wild flowers. Part of the route is linear as the network of unbridged dykes and overgrown areas makes a full circular walk impossible. As one of the longer circuits in the book, it is particularly suitable for older children, especially those who enjoy birdwatching, so remember to take some binoculars. There are lots of colourful waterbirds, including herons, tiny warblers and pipits in the reed beds. Halfway round, there's a short distance along a quiet country lane passing through pretty West Stourmouth.

Getting there *Grove Ferry is just off the A28 between Canterbury and Thanet and is signposted at Upstreet (between Hersden and Sarre). The pub and nature reserve car park are a short distance along Grove Ferry Road. Go over a level crossing and shortly turn left at the wooden sign into the approach road.*

Length of walk 3 miles.
Time 2–2½ hours.
Terrain Flat, comfortable walking, mostly on wide tracks.
Start/parking The nature reserve car park off Grove Ferry Road,

Upstreet. Go over a level crossing and shortly turn left at the wooden sign into the approach road. The car park is to your right up the approach road and costs 50p to £1 (honesty box) (GR 234631). Alternatively, customers of the Grove Ferry Inn can use their car park whilst doing the walk. Keep straight ahead for the pub car park.
Map OS Explorer 150.
Refreshments Grove Ferry Inn is a picturesque, child-friendly pub, located beside the lovely River Stour. It was once a coaching house and today, it has relaxing riverside terraces, colourful gardens and a playground. The

◆ Fun Things to See and Do ◆

Apart from enjoying Grove Ferry Inn's playground and feeding the ever-hungry ducks, the children will love exploring the nature reserve by water. River trips on the Great Stour can be taken from Grove Ferry Inn in a unique paddle steamer. The *Monarch* is 42 ft long, weighs 9 tons and carries up to twelve people. Its steam engine is run by an oil-fired boiler. The trips take 45 minutes and the children can look out for all sorts of interesting wildlife, including stoats, kingfishers and herons. For further details of prices and times, email: **info@leisuresteam.co.uk.** or telephone: 01305 760648.

landlord says to remind the children to bring some bread to feed the ducks. Apparently, they are always very hungry, so please don't disappoint them! Telephone: 01227 860302.

Alternatively, there is a picnic area by the nature reserve car park, with bench tables for those who like to take their own goodies.

The Walk

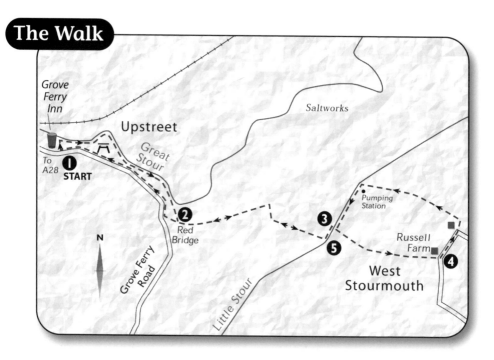

1 The walk begins from the far end of the nature reserve car park, where you bear left across the picnic site and climb a small slope. Pass between two wooden posts waymarked 'Saxon Shore Way and Stour Valley Walk' onto a footpath next to the river.

Continue with the Great Stour on your left until you pass a boatyard on your left, where the narrow footpath drops down onto a wider track. Continue in the same direction, passing through a gate ahead and crossing the driveway to 'The Boatyard', a house with a deep-pitched roof (a good landmark for your return journey). Grove Ferry Road runs on your right, but almost immediately, turn left through metal barriers beside a metal gate onto a wide farm track.

2 Follow the track which shortly curves right, then left, with two farm buildings to the right. Lovely open farmland stretches to either side. Soon, continue with a tree line to your right. When you glimpse a small waterway on your left, turn right, following the tree line, waymarked. Almost immediately, ignore the next right turn, instead following the path ahead, slightly angled left, across fields. At a T-junction of paths, turn left, waymarked on a wooden post, and shortly turn right, crossing a bridge over the Little Stour.

3 Continue straight ahead, with a waterway on your left, and pass a signpost for the Stour Valley Walk. Go between wire fencing on your left and orchards to your right. Soon the dyke runs on your left again. Continue till you reach a quiet

The Monarch paddle steamer (courtesy of Carole Scott).

country lane in West Stourmouth and turn left, watching for occasional traffic.

4 Go past cottages on your left and a farm called Applecroft on your right. Ignore a right turn signed 'Brewery Square'. Soon, turn left down a concrete path by a wooden telephone pylon, passing between houses, then crossing open fields. The path goes over a dyke, then over the Little Stour, with a pumping station on your left. At the main intersecting path turn left. Pass and ignore the bridge you crossed on your outward journey. About 50 yards past this bridge, you'll see the track to the right, through the fields, used earlier.

5 Retrace your steps to the farm gate and metal barrier by the deep-pitched house, 'The Boatyard', which is now in clear view. Cross its driveway and go through the wooden kissing gate. Take the grassy track ahead, keeping the tree line to your left to vary your walk through the picnic area back to the car park and pub.

◆ Background Notes ◆

The Great Stour and the Wantsum Channel separate the Isle of Thanet from the mainland and have been used as shipping routes since the Romans invaded Kent. Forts at Reculver and Richborough were built to guard these important waterways. The pretty village of West Stourmouth, visited halfway round the walk, is actually where the river once met the sea. Stourmouth was under water in Roman times.

18
Reculver

Fun on the beach

The ruins of the Saxon church at Reculver.

This is the walk with everything – the sea, a lovely, light shingle beach, fields and marshlands, sparkling waterways, a ruined abbey in a stunning coastal setting, comfy places to eat and drink, a fascinating visitor centre and a playground for toddlers. Even if you can't complete the circuit because you have a buggy, a linear walk along the level sea wall is delightful as you can still look over the marshes and enjoy the sea-view. There is easy access to the beach and an abundance of fascinating wildlife.

The marshes are an ideal place for spotting large flocks of swans and geese. The sight of swans in flight is amazing, and so is the gentle whirring sound made by the flapping of their enormous wings. Moorhens scurry in the reeds and the tiny, piping trills of warblers and pipits can be heard as you walk through the marshes. Best of all, you can see for miles around while the sky spreads over your head like a huge dome – an appealing aspect of walking in flat country.

18

Getting there *Reculver Country Park is on the north Kent coast 3 miles east of Herne Bay and can be accessed from the A299 (Thanet Way).*

Length of walk 2½ miles.
Time 1½–2 hours.
Terrain Flat, easy walking. The sea wall is ideal for buggies if you don't mind a linear walk,

but the circular walk is not suitable for them.
Start/parking The pay and display car park whose entrance is opposite the King Ethelbert Inn at Reculver (GR 228694).
Map OS Explorer 150.
Refreshments The King Ethelbert Inn is a child-friendly pub, with a varied menu, Telephone: 01227 374368. Also, there is a small café if you turn to your right as you exit the car park.

The Walk

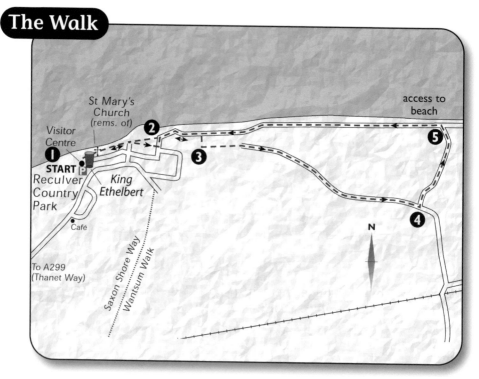

Reculver

1 Leave the car park by the main entrance in the direction of the Reculver towers. Turn left in front of the King Ethelbert Inn, then right to climb the small hill passing the towers on your left. Go down the other side of the hill, where a caravan park faces you. Turn left along the lane towards the sea wall. (Before turning, you may want to look at the ancient Roman wall to the old fort, which runs to the right.)

2 Turn right along the sea wall and, when you reach a green railing on your right enclosing waterworks, turn right alongside it and pass through an opening beside a gate. At the end of the railings, turn left along a wide grassy track.

3 A canal runs to your right and you will see the buildings and waterways of an oyster farm to your left. Take care here, especially if you have younger children, because the wide footpath runs along a ridge and the steep banks of the canal are unprotected. Continue ahead, with canals running left and right. Soon, from the canal to your right, another canal runs away at a right-angle through the fields and marshes. Ignore a dipping track to your left which only goes to the waterway. Pass a point on your right where a straight canal runs at right-angles away from you. Here you may see swans basking in the sunshine on the water or in the fields. For a while, thick reed beds obscure the canal on your left. Pass a pond on your left, and then another pond a little further away. This is the time to use your binoculars as these ponds are teeming with waterbirds.

◆ Fun Things to See and Do ◆

Why not collect some beautiful pebbles and shells from the beach? Perhaps later you could arrange them in a basket or bowl to make a table decoration. A few gulls' feathers might add some interest to the display if you can find any lying around. After all, the gulls won't need them any more!

4 After passing groups of rectangular ponds and criss-crossing waterways on your left, turn left along another grassy footpath. As you approach the sea wall, continue to enjoy wonderful views across fields and marshes. The buildings to your right are on the seafront at Minnis Bay.

5 At the sea wall, turn left towards the Reculver towers. Look out for cormorants sitting on posts emerging from the sea, good vantage points for fishing and for stretching and drying their glossy wings. The children can enjoy themselves on the beach here, which is mostly light shingle with sandy patches. When you decide to continue towards the towers, on reaching the end of the sea wall, go through the gap beside the gate and past the green railings now on your left. Turn left by the caravan park, and, almost immediately, turn right towards the towers, up and over the little hill and back to the starting point.

◆ Background Notes ◆

Reculver's Roman fort dates from the third century and was, originally, almost two miles from the shore. However, the sea is eroding the coastline and now half the fort area has been lost although remains of its great wall survive and can be seen on the walk. During the 1960s eleven skeletons of babies were found beneath the walls during a dig – presumed to be an ancient sacrifice to strengthen the structure.

The beautiful **Reculver towers** are the ruins of St Mary's, a Saxon church, built in the middle of the fort area. The main part of the church was demolished in 1809 before it collapsed into the sea, but it was decided to save the towers, a valuable navigational aid. Today, the towers teeter right on the edge of the coastline, although new defences were built in the 1990s to save them from being swallowed up by the sea which is encroaching at approximately one to two metres a year.

19

Samphire Hoe

An area of outstanding recycling

The winding path at Samphire Hoe.

This is a stunningly beautiful walk, gentle enough for most people yet full of marvellous sights and surprises. The magnificent chalk cliffs of Dover present an ideal backdrop to this amazing place created entirely from the leftover soil excavated to construct the Channel Tunnel. As you walk between the white cliffs and the sparkling sea, it's hard to believe that your surroundings, alive with a variety of birds, butterflies and plants, were once far below the swirling waters of the English Channel.

Volunteer rangers help manage the site and keep it perfect for everybody and are always willing to share information about the short, but fascinating history of the area. Now many birds nest here, including skylarks, meadow pipits and mallards, and you might also spot moorhens, warblers and swallows from the 130 varieties that visit, so binoculars are a must. There are grasshoppers and crickets among the thriving vegetation, while dragonflies and damselflies breed in the ponds.

Kiddiwalks in Kent

19

Getting there *Access to the starting point is off the A20. Driving from Dover to Folkestone, Samphire Hoe is signposted left and you will reach the site via a tunnel through the cliff. (The A20 is dual-carriageway at this point, and on leaving, you will need to turn left. If you wish to return in the Dover direction, leave the A20 at the Capel le Ferne exit and use the roundabout.)*

Length of walk 1¼ miles.
Time 45 minutes to 1 hour.
Terrain Easy flat walking, apart from a short uphill climb. Accessible for pushchairs and buggies.
Start/parking The pay and display car park at Samphire Hoe (GR 293391).
Map OS Explorer 138.
Refreshments There is a kiosk at the Hoe where you can buy hot and cold drinks and snacks. Telephone: 01304 225688.

The Walk

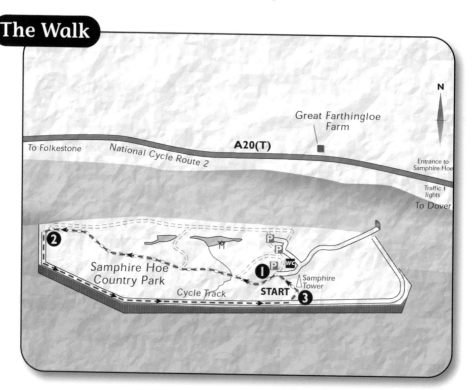

Samphire Hoe

❶ Go to the wooden signpost in the corner of the front car park, waymarked 'West Shore via the Hoe', passing through wooden barriers. There is a picnic area to your right. Keep to this curving tarmac path, with lovely sea views to your left and the magnificent Shakespeare Cliffs to your right. Cross a wooden bridge and ascend slightly for a short while. Soon, the path flattens out, and you will start descending. Don't forget to look out for meadow pipits and skylarks – this is their ideal habitat. Facing you diagonally right, you can see the opening to the railway tunnel through the cliffs that runs between Dover and Folkestone. Continue, keeping to the path and cross a wooden bridge over a lagoon, which is a stretch of salty water separated from the sea. This is an ideal place to look upwards and appreciate the magnificence of the rugged cliffs towering above you.

◆ Fun Things to See and Do ◆

 After you have enjoyed your walk you could visit the Samphire Tower at the edge of the car park, near the sea wall. This work of art was inspired by lighthouses and wooden-clad fishing sheds. Inside there are illustrations on the walls and a telescope for the children to use. As the telescope is moved, it activates different soundscapes depending on where it is pointing. The tower is the perfect place to imagine being a lighthouse-keeper scanning the horizon for ships in distress.

On your return along the sea wall, see how many lighthouses you can spot ahead of you. The answer is at the end of this chapter.

There are plenty of shiny pebbles for the children to collect on the beach

❷ You will see ahead, a delightful bay with a fine shingle beach, just the other side of the sea wall. Turn left along the sea wall, waymarked 'To Car Park via Sea Wall'. Follow the sea wall curving left. The outer sea wall has a concrete barrier, but the pathway is widely-terraced all the way for the return journey. If you climb the shallow steps and use the top terrace, the children will have a lovely view across the bay to the horizon.

❸ At the end of the sea wall, just in front of the blue replica wooden lighthouse, you can turn left along a zigzag path back to the car park. Why not visit the information kiosk to find out what might be on offer in the future?

Samphire Hoe

◆ Background Notes ◆

The White Cliffs of Dover are designated as an Area of Outstanding Natural Beauty, and Samphire Hoe is owned by Eurotunnel and managed in partnership with the White Cliffs Countryside Project. In 1994, a competition was arranged by Eurotunnel, together with the *Dover Express* to name the new site. Mrs Gillian Janaway suggested Samphire Hoe and this became the winning entry. The name derives from samphire, a plant, and 'hoe' which means a piece of land sticking out into the sea. Rock samphire still grows here and you can see a picture of it on the information board. Many years ago local people used to lower themselves down the cliffs on ropes to collect its leaves, a highly dangerous practice. The leaves were sent to London where they were regarded as a delicacy to be served with meat.

It is claimed that, once, a captured highwayman, destined to be imprisoned in Dover Castle, escaped from his guard by pointing in the opposite direction to distract them. While they were looking the other way, the quick-thinking felon climbed down a rope left by a samphire-gatherer. He was never seen again!

The great thing about this country park is that lots of good things are on offer for children during holiday periods. Even better, these regular holiday events are free of charge and come under the general title 'The Green Gang'. For promotional literature on guided walks and events, telephone the White Cliffs Countryside Project on 01304 241806. To talk to the site manager, you can telephone direct on 01304 225649.

Counting Lighthouses – answer:
Looking towards Dover on your return along the sea wall, there are three whole lighthouses visible on the harbour wall and just the top of a fourth. On a clear day the red Varne lightship is also visible.

20

Pegwell Bay Nature Reserve

In the footsteps of England's invaders

The replica Viking ship at Pegwell Bay.

Pegwell Bay Nature Reserve

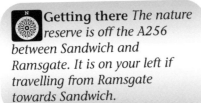

Getting there *The nature reserve is off the A256 between Sandwich and Ramsgate. It is on your left if travelling from Ramsgate towards Sandwich.*

Length of walk 1 mile.
Time 45 minutes to 1 hour.
Terrain Flat, easy walking but bumpy surfaces, so buggies at your own discretion.
Start/parking National Trust pay and display car park,

Pegwell Bay Nature Reserve (GR 342634).
Map OS Explorer 150.
Refreshments There is normally a snack bar selling hot and cold food and ice cream at the starting point but opening times vary according to the season. You may picnic on the site or, alternatively, visit the Sportsman pub on the main road. Turn right out of the car park entrance. The pub is within walking distance, on your right. Telephone: 01843 852547.

The Walk

To Ramsgate   Viking Ship

N

The Sportsman

A256

St Augustine's Golf Club

Ebbsfleet Lane

Cottinghon Hill

Caff Pools

START

Ebbsfleet

1

4

Pegwell Bay

Sandwich Road

Thanet Coastal Path

Ebbsfleet Farm

Pegwell Bay Nature Reserve

Hide

Pegwell Bay Country Park **3**

2

Stonelees Golf Club

Kiddiwalks in Kent

This is a delightful walk, especially if it's a fine day with the sea sparkling like diamonds beyond the salt marshes stretching to its edge. The children will enjoy trying to spot the enormous ferries making their way to Ramsgate harbour and, later, they can visit a superb life-size Viking ship. The nature reserve is an ideal place to do some bird spotting and, if you sit in the bird hide long enough, the children may see plovers, little terns and hen harriers, so don't forget the binoculars. Wading birds and ducks live around the lagoons passed towards the end of the return journey.

In the reserve, you may see Highland cattle and wild Polish ponies grazing. The animals are sometimes moved around so, occasionally, new fences are put up and taken down. However, this part of the reserve is fairly contained and it's easy to gain access to the main coastal path from anywhere in the area.

Plenty of picnic spots and a chance to treat everyone to an ice cream at the end of the outing should make this circuit a favourite.

◆ Fun Things to See and Do ◆

The Viking ship is a beautiful sight and well worth a closer look. It is called the *Hugin* and was a special gift from the *Daily Mail* newspaper, to the people of Ramsgate and Broadstairs. Originally, Vikings were pirates who came from Scandinavia (Finland, Denmark and Sweden) to raid our shores in their longships. Later, they started conquering other lands rather than simply plundering them. After settling in England, a king of Denmark, named Canute, succeeded to the English throne. Do the children know the story about King Canute? It is said that Canute became annoyed at his silly, fawning courtiers, so he performed a demonstration commanding the tide to go out to show them that even a king was not all-powerful.

Pegwell Bay Nature Reserve

Making friends.

1 The nature reserve has an irregularly-shaped car park, but you can see the coastline from its central path so make your way towards it. At the coastal path, turn right and pass through an opening by a gate next to a litterbin shaped like a hut. Follow this narrow footpath, enjoying views to your left across salt marshes towards the rolling waves of Pegwell Bay. The children may see the enormous ferries docking at Ramsgate harbour so it's a good idea to have binoculars handy. After enjoying the view, follow the pathway straight ahead and pass a hide on your right, where you may wish to stop for some birdwatching.

2 As you continue, you will see to your right, towering above everything else, the three enormous cooling towers and tall chimney of Richborough Power Station. Soon, to your left, a canal snakes towards you through the salt marsh. As you follow the path ahead, curving to the right, the power station no longer appears on your right, but faces you, slightly to the left. Ignore the first grassy track to your right. Soon, walk alongside a wire fence around a field on your right. At the apex of the field, follow the fencing round to the right at a 45° angle, for your return journey.

3 Follow this wide, grassy path, ignoring a blue and red banded signpost to the right and, as you start to cross an intersecting footpath, look for two wooden posts facing you, set slightly left. Go between the posts and follow the footpath, bearing right at a small fork and passing through copses before curving right again. Go between two more wooden posts, and you'll see the coast ahead of you. Aim for the coastal path, turn left and retrace your steps for a short way, but do not turn left by the information board into the car park.

4 Continue straight ahead along the main path, and you will see some lagoons on your right. At the lagoons, and just before you reach Sandwich Road, turn left along a wide grassy track and after a few yards, turn left again. The car park is straight ahead.

◆ Background Notes ◆

Pegwell Bay Nature Reserve, along with Sandwich Bay, is owned by the National Trust and managed by the Kent Wildlife Trust. A great number of waders and wildfowl, both migratory and resident, depend on the area for support. Other birdlife includes short-eared owls and snow buntings and in some parts of the reserve, a variety of wild orchids can be found. The **Viking ship** can be found by leaving the nature reserve car park, turning right and driving for ¾ mile. If the large car park is open (hours are irregular), you can turn right and drive in, otherwise there is alternative parking down side-roads to your left. The ship is a replica of the one that sailed from Denmark to Thanet in 1949 to celebrate the 1,500th anniversary of the invasion of our shores when the Saxons arrived in AD 449, although the Vikings themselves did not actually put in an appearance until the 8th or 9th century.

Lagoons are stretches of salt water separated from the sea by a sandbank and are important feeding grounds for wild ducks and wading birds. The lagoons hereabouts are known as 'the caff pools' because a café once stood on the site of the nearby garage.